T0173073

Suzanne M. Ward
Yem S. Fong
Tammy Nickelson Dearie
Editors

Information Delivery in the 21st Century: Proceedings of the Fourth International Conference on Fee-Based Information Services in Libraries

Information Delivery in the 21st Century: Proceedings of the Fourth International Conference on Fee-Based Information Services in Libraries has been co-published simultaneously as *Journal of Interlibrary Loan, Document Delivery & Information Supply*, Volume 10, Number 1 1999.

Pre-publication REVIEWS, COMMENTARIES, EVALUATIONS . . .

"**T**his book is an excellent overview of the issues and realities of fee-based information services in academic and public libraries. . . . It is especially insightful for public libraries considering fee-based services. . . An excellent addition to any library's collection"

Kathy Gillespie Tomajko, MLn, BS
Department Head
Reference Services
Georgia Institute of Technology
Library and Information Center
Atlanta, Georgia

The Haworth Information Press
An Imprint of
The Haworth Press, Inc.

Information Delivery in the 21st Century: Proceedings of the Fourth International Conference on Fee-Based Information Services in Libraries

Information Delivery in the 21st Century: Proceedings of the Fourth International Conference on Fee-Based Information Services in Libraries has been co-published simultaneously as *Journal of Interlibrary Loan, Document Delivery & Information Supply*, Volume 10, Number 1 1999.

The *Journal of Interlibrary Loan, Document Delivery & Information Supply*™ Monographic "Separates"

(formerly the Journal of Interlibrary Loan & Information Supply)*

For information on previous issues of the Journal of Interlibrary Loan & Information Supply series, edited by Leslie R. Morris, please contact: The Haworth Press, Inc., 10 Alice Street, Binghamton, NY 13904-1580 USA.

Below is a list of "separates," which in serials librarianship means a special issue simultaneously published as a journal issue or double-issue *and* as a "separate" hardbound monograph. (This is a format which we also call a "DocuSerial.")

"Separates" are published because specialized libraries or professionals may wish to purchase a specific thematic issue by itself in a format which can be separately cataloged and shelved, as opposed to purchasing the journal on an on-going basis. Faculty members may also more easily consider a "separate" for classroom adoption.

"Separates" are carefully classified separately with the major book jobbers so that the journal tie-in can be noted on new book order slips to avoid duplicate purchasing.

You may wish to visit Haworth's website at . . .

http://www.haworthpressinc.com

. . . to search our online catalog for complete tables of contents of these separates and related publications.

You may also call 1-800-HAWORTH (outside US/Canada: 607-722-5857), or Fax 1-800-895-0582 (outside US/Canada: 607-771-0012), or e-mail at:

getinfo@haworthpressinc.com

Information Delivery in the 21st Century: Proceedings of the Fourth International Conference on Fee-Based Information Services in Libraries

Suzanne M. Ward
Yem S. Fong
Tammy Nickelson Dearie
Editors

Information Delivery in the 21st Century: Proceedings of the Fourth International Conference on Fee-Based Information Services in Libraries has been co-published simultaneously as *Journal of Interlibrary Loan, Document Delivery & Information Supply*, Volume 10, Number 1 1999.

The Haworth Information Press
An Imprint of
The Haworth Press, Inc.
New York • London • Oxford

Information Delivery in the 21st Century: Proceedings of the Fourth International Conference on Fee-Based Information Services in Libraries has also been published as *Journal of Interlibrary Loan, Document Delivery & Information Supply*, Volume 10, Number 1 1999.

The development, preparation, and publication of this work has been undertaken with great care. However, the publisher, employees, editors, and agents of The Haworth Press and all imprints of The Haworth Press, Inc., including The Haworth Medical Press and Pharmaceutical Products Press, are not responsible for any errors contained herein or for consequences that may ensue from use of materials or information contained in this work. Opinions expressed by the author(s) are not necessarily those of The Haworth Press, Inc.

The Haworth Press, Inc., 10 Alice Street, Binghamton, NY 13904-1580 USA

Cover design by Thomas J. Mayshock Jr.

Library of Congress Cataloging-in-Publication Data

International Conference on Fee-based Information Services in Libraries (4th : 1997 : San Diego, Calif.)
    Information delivery in the 21st century : proceedings of the Fourth International Conference on Fee-based Information Services in Libraries / Suzanne M. Ward, Yem S. Fong, Tammy Nickelson Dearie, editors.
        p. cm.
    Includes bibliographical references and index.
    ISBN 0-7890-0839-4 (alk. paper)–ISBN 0-7890-0950-1
    1. Fee-based library services–United States–Congresses. 2. Fee-based library services–Congresses. I. Ward, Suzanne M. II. Fong, Yem S. III. Dearie, Tammy Nickelson. IV. Title

Z683.I58 1997
025.1´1–dc21
                                                            99-054006
                                                                CIP

INDEXING & ABSTRACTING

Contributions to this publication are selectively indexed or abstracted in print, electronic, online, or CD-ROM version(s) of the reference tools and information services listed below. This list is current as of the copyright date of this publication. See the end of this section for additional notes.

- *Academic Abstracts/CD-ROM*
- *Academic Search: data base of 2,000 selected academic serials, updated monthly*
- *BUBL Information Service. An Internet-based Information Service for the UK higher education community <URL:http://bubl.ac.uk/>*
- *CNPIEC Reference Guide: Chinese National Directory of Foreign Periodicals*
- *Current Awareness Abstracts of Library & Information Management Literature, ASLIB (UK)*
- *IBZ International Bibliography of Periodical Literature*
- *Index to Periodical Articles Related to Law*
- *Information Reports & Bibliographies*
- *Information Science Abstracts*
- *Informed Librarian, The*
- *INSPEC*
- *Journal of Academic Librarianship: Guide to Professional Literature, The*
- *Konyvtari Figyelo-Library Review*
- *Library Association Health Libraries Groups, supplement to Health Libraries Review, official journal of LAHLG. Published quarterly by Blackwell Science.*
- *Library & Information Science Abstracts (LISA)*
- *Library & Information Science Annual (LISCA)*

(continued)

- *Library Literature*

- *MasterFILE: updated database from EBSCO Publishing*

- *Newsletter of Library and Information Services*

- *PASCAL*

- *Referativnyi Zhurnal (Abstracts Journal of the All-Russian Institute of Scientific and Technical Information)*

- *Sage Public Administration Abstracts (SPAA)*

Special Bibliographic Notes related to special journal issues (separates) and indexing/abstracting:

- indexing/abstracting services in this list will also cover material in any "separate" that is co-published simultaneously with Haworth's special thematic journal issue or DocuSerial. Indexing/abstracting usually covers material at the article/chapter level.

- monographic co-editions are intended for either non-subscribers or libraries which intend to purchase a second copy for their circulating collections.

- monographic co-editions are reported to all jobbers/wholesalers/approval plans. The source journal is listed as the "series" to assist the prevention of duplicate purchasing in the same manner utilized for books-in-series.

- to facilitate user/access services all indexing/abstracting services are encouraged to utilize the co-indexing entry note indicated at the bottom of the first page of each article/chapter/contribution.

- this is intended to assist a library user of any reference tool (whether print, electronic, online, or CD-ROM) to locate the monographic version if the library has purchased this version but not a subscription to the source journal.

- individual articles/chapters in any Haworth publication are also available through the Haworth Document Delivery Service (HDDS).

ABOUT THE EDITORS

Suzanne M. Ward has worked at the Purdue University Libraries since 1987, first in the Technical Information Service, and since 1993 as Head, Access Services. She was previously head of the Engineering Library at Memphis State University. She holds degrees from UCLA, the University of Michigan, and Memphis State University.

JAI Press published her book *Starting and Managing Fee-Based Information Services in Academic Libraries* in 1997. Her articles about fee-based information services have appeared in publications such as *Marketing News, Advances in Library Resource Sharing, Business Information Alert, MLS: Marketing Library Services, Fee for Service*, and *The Reference Librarian*.

Yem S. Fong is currently Head of Information Delivery Services at the University of Colorado at Boulder Libraries, and also manages the fee-based service, the Colorado Technical Research Center (CTRC). She has been a manager of reference and interlibrary loan services for public, academic and special libraries. She has been a consultant on statewide interlibrary loan and fee-based services projects, and has been a partner in an information brokerage firm. Her degrees are from the University of Colorado, the University of California at Berkeley, and the Japan-America Institute of Management.

She is the author of numerous articles including The Haworth Press, Inc. special issue of the *Journal of Library Administration*, "Interlibrary Loan/ Document Delivery and Customer Satisfaction: Strategies for Redesigning Services."

Tammy Nickelson Dearie is Director of Access & Delivery Services at the University of California Digital Library, Patron Initiated Requesting project. Ms. Dearie is also Director of the UCSD Corporate Programs service and a consultant for fee-based and interlibrary loan services. Engaged in library management and resource sharing for over 11 years, she is the author of several articles on fee-based services, interlibrary loan, and resource sharing. Ms. Dearie is active in many professional organizations including the OCLC Resource Sharing Advisory Committee, incoming Chair of the ACRL Copyright Committee, and a member of the editorial board of the annual review, *ILL/DD: Studies in Interlibrary Loan, Document Delivery, Access Services, and Resource Sharing*.

Information Delivery in the 21st Century: Proceedings of the Fourth International Conference on Fee-Based Information Services in Libraries

CONTENTS

Introduction

Suzanne M. Ward
Yem S. Fong
Tammy Nickelson Dearie

The first fee-based information services in libraries appeared in the 1960's, mostly in academic institutions. Since then, dozens of services have been established in all types of library settings: academic, public, and special. These fee-based services are of all sizes and configurations, but they all share the same mission: providing value-added research services and/or document delivery services to customers on a fee basis. These value-added services are ones that the parent organization cannot afford to offer as part of the standard or basic free library services. Without a fee-based service, these customers, typically businesspeople, would have to look elsewhere for information fulfillment.

Formal research and investigation into fee-based information services are relatively scanty in comparison with other areas of librarianship. Perhaps part of the reason for this dearth of information is be-

Suzanne M. Ward is Head of Access Services at Purdue University Libraries.

Yem S. Fong is Associate Professor and Head, Information Delivery Services, University of Colorado at Boulder, Campus Box 184, Boulder.

Tammy Nickelson Dearie is Director of Access & Delivery Services, University of California at San Diego.

The editors would like to acknowledge the special assistance of Catherine Holdeman, Administrative Assistant, Social Science & Humanities Library, University of California, San Diego.

[Haworth co-indexing entry note]: "Introduction." Ward, Suzanne M., Yem S. Fong, and Tammy Nickelson Dearie. Co-published simultaneously in *Journal of Interlibrary Loan, Document Delivery & Information Supply* (The Haworth Information Press, an imprint of The Haworth Press, Inc.) Vol. 10, No. 1, 1999, pp. 1-3; and: *Information Delivery in the 21st Century: Proceedings of the Fourth International Conference on Fee-Based Information Services in Libraries* (ed: Suzanne M. Ward, Yem S. Fong, and Tammy Nickelson Dearie) The Haworth Press, Inc., 1999, pp. 1-3. Single or multiple copies of this article are available for a fee from The Haworth Document Delivery Service [1-800-342-9678, 9:00 a.m. - 5:00 p.m. (EST). E-mail address: getinfo@haworthpressinc.com].

1

cause fee-based services operate much more closely to a business model than to a library model. Another reason may be that the professionals managing fee-based services, essentially small businesses, are so busy meeting customer information needs that they have little time to write about their experiences.

However, the interest in fee-based services continues to grow for two major reasons. One is that managers of established services continually look for ways to improve the information products they provide, to expand their client base, to forge strategic alliances with other organizations, and to stay abreast of trends in the information and technology explosions. Secondly, the concept of fee-based services, that of meeting customers' needs that go beyond what basic or standard library services can provide, continues to interest librarians and library administrators. Starting a fee-based service, like starting a small business, can be a daunting task. Newcomers glean the literature for "how to" information and contact practitioners for tips.

Since 1983, four conferences on fee-based information services have been held to respond to this ongoing need for practitioners to hone their skills and for newcomers to learn the basics. The first two (at Long Island University in 1983 and at the University of Michigan in 1987) issued conference proceedings. The third conference, held in 1992 with the joint sponsorship of Arizona State University and the Association of Research Libraries, published no proceedings. This special volume contains papers from many of the sessions presented at the Fourth International Conference on Fee-Based Information Services in Libraries held in San Diego in 1997 under the auspices of the University of California at San Diego.

To meet attendees' expectations, the conference planners carefully selected sessions balancing the needs of newcomers with those of established practitioners. The all-day pre-conference workshop, Foundations for Success: Planning a Fee-Based Service from Proposal to Opening Day, led by Steve Coffman (representing the public library view) and Helen Josephine (academic libraries) laid the groundwork for newcomers. The following two days of the conference offered a variety of general sessions and breakout workshops covering topics from copyright to pricing to business plans.

We are pleased to present these papers from the Fourth International Conference on Fee-Based Information Services in Libraries in the hopes that they will assist information professionals interested in starting new fee-based services or in improving existing fee-based services.

Keynote Address:
Fourth International Conference
on Fee-Based Information Services
in Libraries

Herbert S. White

SUMMARY. Despite the debate over free vs. fee libraries and services, libraries need to accept the responsibility of providing information to our users. Libraries, and fee-based services in libraries, need to lead the way in recognizing the need for libraries, developing the role of librarians as managers of knowledge, and creating our own future. The author makes the argument that knowledge work will be done by *somebody*, and if not us, then the end-user. Providers of fee-based services have already staked out our jurisdiction and are on the right track. *[Article copies available for a fee from The Haworth Document Delivery Service: 1-800-342-9678. E-mail address: getinfo@haworthpressinc.com <Website: http://www.haworthpressinc.com>]*

KEYWORDS. Fee-based information services, future of librarianship, knowledge management, free vs. fee

This is your fourth Conference on Fee Based Services, but only the first I have attended. I am interested to note that the conference pro-

---

Herbert S. White is Distinguished Professor Emeritus and Dean Emeritus, School of Library and Information Science, Indiana University, 330 East El Viento, Green Valley, AZ 85614.

[Haworth co-indexing entry note]: "Keynote Address: Fourth International Conference on Fee-Based Information Services in Libraries." White, Herbert S. Co-published simultaneously in *Journal of Interlibrary Loan, Document Delivery & Information Supply* (The Haworth Information Press, an imprint of The Haworth Press, Inc.) Vol. 10, No. 1, 1999, pp. 5-11; and: *Information Delivery in the 21st Century: Proceedings of the Fourth International Conference on Fee-Based Information Services in Libraries* (ed: Suzanne M. Ward, Yem S. Fong, and Tammy Nickelson Dearie) The Haworth Press, Inc., 1999, pp. 5-11. Single or multiple copies of this article are available for a fee from The Haworth Document Delivery Service [1-800-342-9678, 9:00 a.m. - 5:00 p.m. (EST). E-mail address: getinfo@haworthpressinc.com].

5

gram is primarily devoted to *how* you do what you do, and I will not intrude into a process in which my comments would really be uninformed. I would rather talk about *why* you do what you do, and why it is important that you do it. In addressing this topic, I am aware of some arguments that have been raised as to whether you should be offering fee-based services from libraries at all. It can be contended that fee-based services somehow attack and undermine the provision of free services. The argument is made that once services are provided for a fee, there will be a temptation to withdraw funding. The individuals who make this emotional statement offer no proof of any decision to withdraw already offered free services in order to offer these for a fee. Instead, there is plenty of evidence of reductions in funding without any alternative "temptation" of the kind being charged. Rather, library activities are curtailed because those who fund us would rather not spend the money, and we have offered neither any inducement to change their minds nor the threat of what would happen to them unless they did. The argument that services for a fee replace free services is, in my observation, totally without merit. Service for a fee replaces, for libraries, the absence of services.

However, those who might feel a legitimate concern about this issue must then accept the responsibility for seeing to it that funding for totally free services in all kinds of libraries is increased dramatically, and as you will see from my later remarks there is no real political or economic reason why funding for such *free* library services should not be tripled or quadrupled. There is certainly logic and validity in such a demand: first, because it is worth it for the good of the community being served, and second, because the alternative is ignorance, which occurs when services are offered neither for free nor for a fee, is unacceptable if articulated. If your critics then took the challenge of free instead of fee as a crusade theme to demand and also obtain substantial increases in funding and staffing in both academic and public libraries, there would be no problem.

Indeed, Eugene Garfield's[1] argument that the need for information for the mind is as important as the need for food for the body is worth considering. Garfield has argued for the issuance of information stamps as a government subsidy to be used in libraries, to allow us to keep honest books as grocery stores are allowed to keep honest books when they deliver food in return for food stamps. However, this has not happened, and it is not likely to happen, since we don't even try.

Instead, the slogan "free and not fee" has become "free or not at all." However, "not at all" only means "not by us." We offer no objection when others offer services for a fee, even though this clearly still disqualifies those who cannot pay. The outrage at inequity extends only to our own participation. By providing services for a fee openly and honestly you are at least protecting our professional territory and our birthright. You are attacked because you are honest.

The real betrayers of our profession and of our clients are found in libraries such as the ones that:

1. Agree to the building of more and larger public libraries without demanding additional staffing before the first brick is laid.
2. Agree with the premise that academic libraries must do more with less without even examining what really happens when that nonsensical idea is exposed. What happens is that even greater costs accrue to the institution, but they are hidden and not noticed in various academic budgets. Forcing the president to face the reality that the most cost-effective information access will require a substantial increase in the library budget is the most honest approach. It channels the money to those most competent to manage it. The alternative is simply a free-for-all.
3. Accept new responsibilities in public libraries for additional services, such as literacy programs or student services, simply because the public school or the charter school would rather dump this problem on the public library without additional funding.
4. Allow unqualified people to do professional work in reference or in online searching, particularly while we then do clerical work. Would surgeons, or any other professionals, allow such a scenario?

It is time to state some of the concepts articulated by Peter Drucker, for whose management wisdom I have unbounded admiration, and whose arguments certainly apply to librarians:

1. In the claimed absence of money, there is always money.
2. It is easier to get a lot of money than a little bit of money.
3. In the provision of a service or a product that important people consider essential, its cost is irrelevant, and
4. Your boss is responsible for everything you do and everything you do not do, and once your boss understands the importance of making you more effective, he or she becomes your most important *subordinate*.

It is not in what information for a fee workers do, but in our failure to apply Drucker's principles that we are betrayed. Drucker understands the importance of knowledge as we approach the next millennium, in both real and political terms. The search for knowledge or information has no avowed enemies. There is no pro-stupidity lobby. On the other hand, who actively supports librarians in presenting this argument? Stating that we would support libraries *if* we had money provides only dishonesty, because we will never have enough money to do everything. Peter Drucker has noted that in the political process there are no neutrals. If individuals do not support you as a primary or urgent priority they are enemies, because they are supporting some other priority. How many of our "friends" place the library first, ahead of whatever else they would like to do? Drucker is confident enough in his argument to posit that knowledge workers will be the most important profession of the next century.[2] However, he does not mention librarians, and he does not state who these knowledge workers will be. It is clear that other professions in such areas as business administration and computer systems engineering understand the importance of claiming to be knowledge workers, even if we do not.

By contrast the national newspaper *USA Today* mentions us quite specifically. In an article that identifies fields without a future for new recruits, the newspaper singles out bank tellers, telephone operators, and librarians.[3] The connection, at least in the eyes of the writers, is that these are fields that perform routine and clerical work that will be taken over by computers. We can and should certainly argue that such a characterization is inaccurate and unfair, but then where did *USA Today* get its perception of what librarians do? Probably from watching librarians, and we must all understand the danger that comes from the fact that this newspaper is read by policy- and decision-makers.

There is beginning to be some recognition of a potential role for librarians as knowledge managers, but to a large extent in publications such as *Library Journal* this description is limited to special librarians in the corporate world. To a considerable extent, the role of academic and public librarians in the information process is seen as passive, as collecting and arranging material so that others can locate the information. For many librarians, their abdication suggests not a preference for free over fee, but rather a preference for not at all over either of these alternatives.

Knowledge work will certainly be done by *somebody*, as Peter Drucker predicts. The alternative of ignorance, particularly in a competitive society, is simply not acceptable. However, by whom might this work be done?

1. By us. Your group, in providing this service for a fee, is at least doing what needs to be done. Those who complain that you ought not do this while themselves doing nothing are only stressing their irrelevance.
2. By the end-user. Here we encounter issues involving their qualifications and the cost effectiveness of "delegating" to individuals who, at least in academia and industry, are paid more. However, of even greater concern is their willingness to do this work. When the University of Alberta Libraries set up end-user training workshops for faculty members, only a tiny number registered themselves. A larger number sent their secretaries and other clerical assistants. The greatest number ignored the opportunity.
3. By nobody at all. That option is indeed suggested by the University of Alberta reaction. After all, it is still possible to avoid the search for knowledge because ignorance is rarely admitted and rarely challenged by others. It is still comfortable and safe to pretend to know "everything" that is needed. In my corporate experience, I never encountered a presentation that began with an admission of ignorance.
4. Most probably, by somebody other than either librarians or the end-user. This process may or may not turn out to be cost effective, depending on the qualifications of the provider. However, the fact that an "information for a fee" industry is growing around us is certainly obvious to all of you. The reason is quite simple. Part comes from the laws of physics. Nature abhors a vacuum. The other part comes from Drucker, as noted earlier. For important people to get what they want (or even just what they think they want), the cost is irrelevant. The British business journal *The Economist* points to the development of what is rather charmingly called the Meatware Industry (people as differentiated from hardware and software), and notes that meatware companies are likely to be profitable investments.[4] As noted earlier, in the absence of money there is money. Let's not confuse that truth with the observation that people don't want to give us money.

What then do we accomplish if we refuse to do this work for a fee, while also failing to achieve the funds necessary to allow us to do it for free? We then reduce ourselves to the clerical extinction which *USA Today* predicts. It is also the extinction that some library schools perceive as they seek desperately to jump out of what they see as a leaky and sinking boat into something dryer and safer. Does an insistence on not charging, if it results in not doing the work at all as a matter of principle, help our clients? No. The poor ones won't get served at all, and the others who can afford to pay can certainly find a vast range of other options, including the meatware industry. Such an approach serves nobody–certainly not the poor, certainly not us, and not even affluent clients. We could provide information more cost effectively, as indeed your group does.

For me, the solution for our clients, and of course for ourselves, comes from the acceptance of the work of Andrew Abbott and his book *The System of Professions.*[5] Abbott makes three points that for him, and indeed for me, define any profession and that define ours if indeed we claim to be a profession:

1. The task of professionals is to address human problems amenable to expert service. This is the self-definition of self-styled professionals, from doctors and lawyers to plumbers and garage mechanics. What definition of expert service do we seek to carve out for ourselves?
2. Professionals compete vigorously for existing and newly emerging problem jurisdictions. Can we see the "information-based society" as such a problem jurisdiction?
3. Professionals seek to expand their jurisdictions by preempting the activities of other professions. Do these "others" include the MIS people, information systems analysts? Do they include our encouragement of end-user searching without having the vaguest idea how well they do it?

I believe that Abbott defines our future, if we are to have a future. Your own group has seen the need to stake out and defend your problem jurisdictions, and for this I salute you. I don't see many other librarians, particularly in the public and academic sectors, doing this. They are still promising that they, or at least their unlucky subordinates, will do more with less. However, even if this were possible it would be more clerical work at the expense of our professional jurisdiction. You are on the right track. I congratulate you, and I wish you well.

NOTES

1. Garfield, Eugene. *Essays of an Information Scientist.* Philadelphia, PA: ISI Press, 1977.

2. Drucker, Peter F. *The Post-Capitalist Society.* New York: Harper Business Books, 1993.

3. "Future Jobs to Bank on: Therapists, not Tellers," *USA Today,* 11 April 1996, p. 1D.

4. "Tel-Tech Tales." *The Economist,* 327, no. 7817, p. 90-91. June 26, 1993.

5. Abbott, Andrew D. *The System of Professions. An Essay on the Division of Expert Labor.* Chicago: University of Chicago Press, 1988.

Special Considerations
for Fee-Based Services
in Public Libraries

Steve Coffman

SUMMARY. Public libraries face special challenges in initiating and maintaining successful fee-based services. Major challenges include the fact that, unlike in academic libraries, public libraries have no clearly defined "non-primary clientele" to whom to offer services. Public libraries provide basic services for everyone in their jurisdiction, and often face vocal opposition to establishing a unit offering value-added services on a cost-recovery basis. Legislation may pose additional obstacles. Defining the dividing point between free services and fee services can also be challenging. The author offers advice and insights based on his decade of experience as director of a fee-based service in a large public library. *[Article copies available for a fee from The Haworth Document Delivery Service: 1-800-342-9678. E-mail address: getinfo@ haworthpressinc.com]*

KEYWORDS. Fee-based information services, public libraries, value-added services, cost-recovery, planning, free vs. fee, non-profit, legal issues, County of Los Angeles Public Library

Fee-based information services have traditionally been most closely associated with academic libraries. Many of the earliest services were

Steve Coffman is, Director, FYI, County of Los Angeles Public Library, 12350 Imperial Highway, Norwalk, CA 90650 (Website: http://fyi.co.la.ca.us).

[Haworth co-indexing entry note]: "Special Considerations for Fee-Based Services in Public Libraries." Coffman, Steve. Co-published simultaneously in *Journal of Interlibrary Loan, Document Delivery & Information Supply* (The Haworth Information Press, an imprint of The Haworth Press, Inc.) Vol. 10, No. 1, 1999, pp. 13-28; and: *Information Delivery in the 21st Century: Proceedings of the Fourth International Conference on Fee-Based Information Services in Libraries* (ed: Suzanne M. Ward, Yem S. Fong, and Tammy Nickelson Dearie) The Haworth Press, Inc., 1999, pp. 13-28. Single or multiple copies of this article are available for a fee from The Haworth Document Delivery Service [1-800-342-9678, 9:00 a.m. - 5:00 p.m. (EST). E-mail address: getinfo@haworthpressinc.com].

started by colleges and universities looking for ways to serve a growing number of research firms and other "non-primary clientele" that began showing up in their libraries in the early 1970's asking for online searches, document delivery, and a host of other services that had only been available to faculty and students. Even today, the field continues to be dominated by academic institutions. The current edition of ALA's *Internet Plus Directory of Express Library Services*, which keeps track of fee-based services, lists 192 services in academic libraries and 92 in corporate and special libraries; public libraries trailed with only 77 entries.[1] FISCAL, the ACRL discussion group of Fee-Based Information Services in Academic Libraries and the *de facto* industry "association" has "academic" right in its name. And much of what is said and published on the topic continues to focus on the academic experience.

That said, public libraries have developed some of the most innovative fee-based services in the industry. And successful programs such as NYPL Express at New York Public, the INFORM service which has operated out of the Minneapolis Public Library since 1971, INFO II at the Tulsa Public Library, and the FYI Service at the County of Los Angeles Public Library, all prove that fee-based services can play an important role in public libraries–if they are handled right.

Handling them right means developing and operating services that are designed for the public library environment. For while we share many things in common with our fee-based cousins in academic and special libraries, public libraries also present some special challenges and problems such as the "free vs. fee" issue, legal constraints, and resource and market issues which can kill the best laid plans if they are not taken into account from the beginning. It is my purpose to review some of the more important of these "special considerations for public libraries" with you here, and to discuss some possible solutions and work-arounds that those of us who have been in the business have developed over many years of trial and error.

FEE-BASED SERVICES AND THE FREE PUBLIC LIBRARY

The "free vs. fee" issue is most starkly drawn in the public library arena because we really do not have any "non-primary" clientele as is the case in academic libraries, and because there are some strong long-standing moral objections against fees in the public library community.

I don't want to get into this controversy too deeply, because you have already given a lot of thought to why you want a fee-based service, and to the kind of objections you might encounter. If you have a problem in this area at all it's most likely to come from certain members of your staff or the library profession. The public generally understands and are thankful for the new services.

If the staff or the profession does object, it will probably be with variations on ALA's Policy Statement 50.4 which states that,

> The American Library Association asserts that the charging of fees and levies for information services including those services utilizing the latest information technology is discriminatory in publicly supported institutions providing library and information services.[2] (ALA Handbook of Organization, 1996-1997)

The Public Library Association (PLA) has taken a decidedly more permissive tack in resolutions adopted at its conference in Portland, Oregon in 1997. But many in the library profession still share John Berry's view of fee-based services as outlined in his *Library Journal* editorial, "The Popular Quick Fix, Undermining Library Credibility and Principle," from August 1997.

> The oldest quick fix in libraries is the fee-based service. Despite dozens of failures, and scant evidence that fees ever deliver revenue enough to cover the full cost of the service, they are still a favorite among embattled library administrators. Steve Coffman, the manager of fee-based services at the County of Los Angeles Public Library, is the most visible fee pusher. In L.A. County and many other places, steady budget erosion has added to the pressure to charge for services. Fees haven't helped. Fees relieve librarians of responsibility to involve the public and the staff in the development of services, to defend the rest of the library budget, and to base services on real needs, not market wishes and convenience. They promote very easy bottom-line measures of success, rarely assessing who fails to get or ask for service, or the impact of the fee on access to information. Fees turn the library into a store.[3]

With all due respect to Berry, I've been working with FYI since we first opened our doors in 1988, and over that period I've said a lot of things about fee-based services. But I've never said they are a quick fix. We've been around more than ten years and we are still trying to get them right. Nor do I see them as a significant source of net revenue for libraries, at least not at this time.

However, I see fee-based services as an integral part of modern library service, and I believe those who avoid them on moral grounds do a disservice to their members and their communities.

Let me explain what I mean. At FYI our primary purpose is to allow the library to offer information products and services that would not otherwise be available. Our motto is "The Best Information at the Best Price." Of course, the best price is free, whenever possible, but when it's not possible, we feel we owe it to our patrons to make sure they get the best possible information at the lowest possible cost.

See Figure 1 and Figure 2 to compare traditional library services with libraries that also provide fee-based services. The inside circle represents basic library services, and it appears in both the traditional library model and the fee-based model. Thus, the County of Los Angeles Public Library provides everything John Berry might expect to find in a traditional library and we provide it for free.

FIGURE 1

Traditional Library

Patrons Left to Fend for Themselves

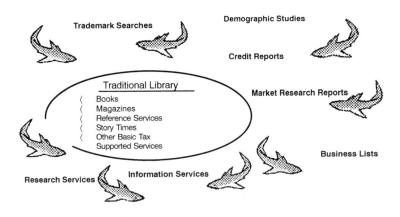

FIGURE 2

Fee-Based Model

Library As Patron's Agent

Fee-Based Services

Traditional Library

(Books
(Magazines
(Reference Services
(Story Times
(Other Basic Tax
  Supported Services

Demographic Studies
Business Credit Reports
Business List Services
Patent Searches
Market Research Reports
Custom Research Services
Trademark Searches
Information Services

The difference is that when the patrons need more than the traditional library can provide for free, such as a trademark search or a business credit report, or any of hundreds of other information products, there is nowhere for them to go and they are left to fend for themselves with the sharks and other ravenous vendors in the information marketplace.

But at L.A. County we wouldn't think of turning our backs on our patrons' information needs. When they ask for patent searches, or trademark searches, or dozens of other products and services, FYI is there to help them by

- Selecting the best information providers available.
- Saving them money (we negotiate best prices, eliminate subscription costs and annual contracts, other prohibitive pricing schemes).
- Giving them honest, unbiased information about the various ways they can solve an information problem.
- Giving them the assistance they need to select the right information for the right job.

Our services are not designed to generate a profit, nor should they be. FYI's primary purpose is to improve access to information and it contradicts that purpose to add on extra fees to generate a profit.

Just so you don't get the idea that this is some deviant philosophy we dreamed up in L.A., let me point out that this same model has been used by all kinds of other public and non-profit institutions for some time now.

Take public education as an example. If there is one institution that is even more critical to the functioning of a democracy than a library, it would have to be public education. Public schools provide free educational services to all the children of our community, using our tax dollars. However, they also provide a range of fee-based services that go beyond the school's basic educational function but that meet additional needs of the students and parents. Examples of these fee-based services include cafeteria lunches, morning and afternoon daycare, and after-school classes such as jewelry making or pet care that don't fit into the standard curriculum. As in a library, these services aren't designed to make a profit, but to offer the programs and services its customers want. Parents who don't want to take advantage of after-school care don't pay for it, just as patrons who don't need value-added research services don't pay for those, either.

You could claim, as Berry and others have, that fees have no place in publicly supported institutions, but you would have a tough time getting anyone in our school district to agree with you. They are just happy that they don't have to get up at the crack of dawn to pack a lunch every day for their kids, and they are happy that there is somebody around here to take care of their children until they get home at 6 p.m.

In short, at the County of Los Angeles Public Library we feel that fee-based services are an integral part of our library services. And we think they can do a lot to help libraries and other institutions provide a broader range of services to their customers. But we do not see them as a panacea for all that ails us, nor as a quick fix, nor as a significant source of revenue for libraries.

So the mission of FYI is to provide the customers of the County of Los Angeles Public Library with the "Best Information at the Best Price." But that is certainly not the only rationale a library might have for starting a fee-based service. Some libraries really hope to generate substantial amounts of revenue, although few have been successful. Others, particularly academic libraries, have started them to serve business people and other "non-primary clientele" in their communities. But the important point here is not so much what your mission is, because that may vary from library to library, but design your service to be consistent with it.

One of the major issues is deciding whether the service should generate a profit, just cover its cost, or be subsidized. For example, if, as at FYI, the primary mission of the service is to provide access to information that would not otherwise be available, then the objective should be to keep the prices as low as possible. A profit-making service would be inconsistent with that mission, particularly if it raised prices above what customers could do on their own at retail. Cost recovery would be all right, but there is nothing that says just because you charge a fee, you have to recover all your costs.

But if you opt for a subsidized service to serve the needs of your community, better be careful that the subsidy is only available to your community. It's amazing how many of us are trying to provide subsidized services to the whole world, in an effort to increase our sales volume.

LEGAL ISSUES

Once you've resolved the ethical and mission issues, most public libraries have to overcome some legal hurdles to provide fee-based services.

In many states, the enabling legislation for public libraries declares, in essence, that "library services shall be forever free to the public." For example, in California, the County of Los Angeles Public Library operates under a section of the Education Code called the County Free Public Libraries Act which includes the word "free" right in the title of the law and states

> The Legislature finds and declares that it is in the interest of the people and of the state that there be a general diffusion of information and knowledge through the continued operation of *free* public *libraries*. Such diffusion is a matter of general concern inasmuch as it is the duty of the state to provide encouragement to the voluntary lifelong learning of the people of the state.[4] (California Education Code Section 18010)

However, despite this wording and the obvious implication that libraries should be free, most public libraries in California, and everywhere, offer some kind of fee-based services, such as photocopying, meeting rooms, book reserves, videos, printing, best seller rentals, pencil sales, and so on. The trick here is to distinguish between the mandated basic library services that are free, and optional or supplementary services that you can charge for.

Here's how we did it when we set up FYI. Look at your governing legislation and see exactly what it says. Also look for any Attorney General interpretations of the legislation (one existed in California) or any court cases that may have been bought on the code sections and related legislation. Pay particular attention to words like "basic services" that may enable you to distinguish between different levels and types of services, some of which you have to provide for free, others which you can charge for.

Next, examine the fees you are already charging, such as for photocopying or meeting room rentals, and find out how these have been justified under current legislation. Some of these fee-based services, like photocopying, have been around for a long time, and so it will not always be easy to locate the original justifications in the old files. If you can't find the original justification, don't worry. The fact that you have an existing fee-based service can serve as an important precedent for you, even if you can't find how it was justified.

Once you've got your governing legislation and information on all your current fees, you've got everything you need to sit down and design your own justification. Your particular approach will be governed by your individual circumstances, but in general you should look for things that let you distinguish between the research, document delivery, and other information products and services you want to provide and the basic library services like reference and circulation. In L.A. County, it was the fact that the customers received a product that was theirs to keep that allowed us to distinguish our fee-based research services from traditional reference where we just answered a question or assisted the patron in using the collection. In other cases justification may be determined by the nature of the service itself; renting meeting rooms, for example, is usually not considered a "basic library service" because it is a function that is also offered elsewhere, such as by hotels and conference centers, and is not unique to libraries. By extension, this same reasoning might serve a library that wanted to rent its videoconferencing equipment out to individuals and businesses for remote job interviews, or teleconferencing applications, or similar types of services.

In most cases, you will find that you have all the rationale you need to establish a wide variety of fee-based services in the library under existing legislation, no matter how onerous it appears to be on the surface. However, it is conceivable that there could be some circumstances where the law simply would not permit the library to charge a fee for particular types of services. If you find yourself in this situation, you still have some options. First, see whether it is feasible to have your Friends group, library foundation, or some other library-related organization charge the fee, rather than the library itself. Many libraries have used this technique in developing their rental video collections, and there is no reason why it should not work in other areas as well. Another option would be to bring in a commercial concession. For example, it may not be permissible for the library to charge for research services, but there may be nothing to prevent you from leasing out part of your space to a commercial information broker and charging rent and a percentage of their revenue in exchange for access to your collections and your patrons. Finally, if none of these options is available, you can always get your governing legislation changed, although this can be a frustrating and time-consuming process, and definitely not an option for the weak of heart.

DRAWING THE LINE BETWEEN FREE AND FEE

Once you've dealt with the difference between free and fee on the legal side, you have to address it from the practical side. How are you going to draw the line between free and fee so that the staff and the public can understand it? Below are some of the many different ways to do this.

Type or Format of Material

Example: "If you want the video of *King Lear* it will cost you $1.50, if you want to read the book you can do it for free."

This type of distinction is frowned upon by both ALA and PLA, and of course, it's the most common type of fee-based service in the library. They have a point; it does seem arbitrary. But I see it as situational ethics: If you have a relatively fixed income for your library, and the only way you can add videos is by cutting back on books, by all means charge for the videos.

Place of Delivery

Example: "If you want to come in and photocopy the article, it's free, if you want us to send it to you, it's $10.00."

Speed or Type of Delivery

Example: "Our ILL service can get you that book in six weeks at no cost, or our document delivery service can get it for you within 48 hours for $20.00 plus courier charges."

Extent of Effort (How Much Time and Money You Can Afford to Spend on a Patron)

Example Time: "We'd be happy to help you research that question if you would care to come in, or, if you prefer, our fee-based service can handle the matter for you."
Example Money: "We can spend up to $25.00 in information costs on your question, after that we will need to charge you."

This is the most difficult area to handle because libraries generally provide some level of the service for free and it becomes fee-based only when it's going to require too much time or cost too much money. You can define the extent of effort explicitly (to an extent, anyway), e.g., "We'll do three of these for free, but the fourth will cost $5.00." Or you can leave it up to the librarians' discretion (at the point where you would normally ask the patron to come in, you can also offer the option of the fee-based service).

Type of Product

Some products and services are simply not offered as part of basic library service, such as credit reports, trademark searches, business lists, books, sandwiches at the library cafeteria, etc.

Type of Customer

Example: If a patron lives or works within the service area, the service is free (or lower cost), but if the patron lives outside there is a fee. Or the service is available at lower rates for non-profit organizations, service is free to city government, fee-based for the general public, and so on.

No matter what your criteria, in order to be able to draw these lines effectively, you need:

- a good definition of your basic services
- a clear understanding of the purpose you want to serve in your fee-based service
- knowledge about what you are legally permitted to charge for.

MANAGING WITH LIMITED RESOURCES

Most public library fee-based services operate out of major urban public libraries. While many smaller libraries may have wanted to open a service, many have shied away from it because they are afraid they don't have what it takes to pull them off. That is, they are afraid that their collections are not large enough to support real research, that they lack the databases and other electronic resources their customers will want, that they lack staff with the required expertise, or that the whole library may simply be spread too thin.

Those are all good reasons to be cautious, but just because you are a small- or medium-sized library doesn't mean it's impossible. There are some tested business models that work for smaller libraries.

- *Specialization.* You can specialize. If you have a special collection or resource that will justify it, operate a service that specializes in that area. For example, the Pasadena Historical Society has a great collection of old photographs of the city that they sell to law offices, film companies, interior decorators and others for a profit. Many libraries have special collections of a similar nature that they might be able to market. Other good examples of specialization are the SCI3 Patent Library of the Sunnyvale Public Library, the American Bankers Association Research Service, the Gambling Collection at the University of Nevada, Las Vegas, and many others.

  Of course, specialization often requires reaching beyond your own community to find an adequate customer base, and that requires good marketing, which often requires money. But if your business case is good, it can justify the investment in marketing.

- *Partnerships*. You can partner with other services in larger libraries. You can set up a service that runs with a small staff locally, and then partner with other larger institutions for access to their collections, resources, and staff expertise. In this case, it's good to have something that you excel in locally, both to maintain your service's identity and so that you have something to sell to other institutions.

- *Outsourcing*. Finally, you can outsource your entire fee-based service if you want to. A great example of this is the Public Radio Music Source run by Minnesota Public Broadcasting. They developed a service that allows public radio customers to purchase any music they've heard on any participating public radio station in the United States simply by calling an 800 number. Participating stations advertise the service and send all their play lists to Minnesota Public Radio. Minnesota Public Radio takes all the orders, handles warehousing, fulfillment, and all of the other business details, and gives participating stations a percentage of every sale they generate. We tried this approach at FYI with a program called Metro Business Services where we provided services to other libraries and gave the libraries a percentage of all the sales they generated. However, it was not very effective. We feel the primary reason was that the service was not tightly integrated with basic library services, so that the librarians behind the reference desk did not always know what products and services were available. Secondly, the small- to medium-sized companies that are the primary market for our services were not in the habit of using these libraries for information services of any type. It would have required extensive marketing to convince them to change their minds. So while the outsourcing model does show some potential for development, be aware of the potential problems and be prepared to address them.

SERVING THE SMALLER CUSTOMER

With very few exceptions, public libraries, if they are serving business at all, serve small- to medium-sized businesses. That is both because these smaller firms make up by far the largest number of businesses in our communities and because most larger businesses already have their own sources of information and don't need what we have to offer.

The problem is that most small businesses are run on shoestrings, or rather on their owners' Visa or MasterCard, and they often just don't have the kind of money it takes to afford the typical costs of fee-based services. That is especially true when the information we have to give them does not always justify the price. Many of these businesses would much rather go with the their hunches than pay $150-$200 for a handful of trade journal articles and press releases that tell them little more than they already knew.

So what's the solution? If you want to serve small business, find ways of getting the costs down and the value up. Here are some ways to do that:

- Don't just try to sell what you have. Start with their information needs and find the information you need to serve them.
- Come up with standardized products that are designed to serve those needs. We swear by this approach at FYI for a number of reasons. First, standardized products allow us to put information in context the customer can use. Our trademark searches, for example, include detailed explanations of what the various records mean, information on how to analyze the search, and so forth. They are not just a data dump. Secondly, standardization allows us to reduce both staff and material costs. And finally, products can be developed around prices the business community is willing to pay.

So where do you find these products? You've got two choices. First, you can try to find good products that are already on the market, and make arrangements with the producer to retail them. FYI does this with a number of our products including business lists, certain types of company reports, and demographic products. The important thing to remember if you are retailing somebody else's product is that you've got to buy it wholesale. It's not fair to you or to the customer if you have to charge them the regular shelf price of the product and then tack on some kind of a handling charge to cover your own costs. Negotiate with the vendor for a wholesale rate based on the volume you sell, and then your expenses should come out of the margin between the wholesale and retail prices.

In many cases, however, you will find that there are no products on the market that answer the information needs of your customers, or the product may exist but you can't work out the kind of deal you want with the producer. In either case, you simply have to develop your own, or take something that already exists and enhance it.

But no matter how many products you come up with, they will not answer every question, and so you probably still need to offer custom research services to handle projects that can't be answered by your products. But there are ways to keep your costs down here as well:

- Keep your hourly rates as low as possible. If your purpose is really to serve your local business community, take a look at subsidizing overheads or other aspects of the operation.
- Offer differential rates. Have lower hourly rates for projects that can be handled by paraprofessional staff.
- Keep your project minimums low. Use fifteen-or thirty-minute minimums instead of one hour to reduce the initial cost hurdle to get into a project and to make the service more attractive to small business. Find a way to handle these small projects efficiently, so you don't spend an hour doing the work, billing, and so forth, on a project where you are only getting paid for thirty minutes.
- Average project costs are actually more important than hourly rates, so keep them as low as possible. Consider standardizing a low-cost introductory research package, perhaps based on Internet research, that had a few items in full text, a list of titles, and suggestions and strategies for further research.
- Do whatever you can to reduce the cost of the raw materials, the information that goes into the products and services you provide. There are plenty of alternatives to the traditional online services these days, such as the Internet. However, there is also lots of competition in other areas. For example, you may find it is better to go directly to the source for information you use regularly rather than to buy it from a traditional online service like Dialog. It's a buyer's market and information prices are dropping all the time.
- Lastly, make sure that you provide your community with lots of good, free business information. That's one of the advantages

you have over most of the commercial services that are trying to reach your customers. Most of you are not in business to make money, but to make getting information as easy and as inexpensive as possible for your community. If you offer great free business information services, people will naturally come to you to purchase the supplementary fee-based products as well. If you can deliver, customers will come to trust you with their information needs.

ONWARD

These then, are some of the special problems of operating a fee-based service in a public library. When you add them to all of the normal issues involved in running a fee-based service in any kind of library, such as copyright, licensing, staffing, pricing, billing, collections, copyright, and so on, and then throw in the routine trials and tribulations of getting any new business off the ground, the whole process looks pretty daunting. After over fifteen years of ups and downs and lots of hard work, I know that running a good fee-based service is no walk in the park.

However, many others who have survived in this business can also tell you that although the problems are difficult, they are not insurmountable. If you can manage to get it right, the rewards are great. Fee-based services allow you to provide your community with a range of information products and services that extend far beyond those offered by any traditional free public library service. A fee-based service is evidence of your library's commitment to serving your customers' information needs, whatever they may be. They are proof that you stand as ready to make sure they get a good trademark search or credit report or demographic study or research project at a reasonable price as you are to make sure they have free services such as plenty of books to check out, and knowledgeable staff to answer their reference questions, and storytimes for their children. Developing and operating a library service like that is hardly a "quick fix." It is a difficult and worthy endeavor.

NOTES

1. Coffman, Steve, Cynthia A. Kehoe, and Pat Wiedensohler with the assistance of FYI, County of Los Angeles Public Library, Information Researchers, University of Illinois at Urbana-Champaign, and FISCAL, Fee-Based Information Service Centers in Academic Libraries, a discussion group of the American Library Association of College & Research Libraries/American Library Association. Chicago: American Library Association, 1998. *The Internet-Plus Directory of Express Library Services: Research and Document Delivery for Hire.*

2. ALA Handbook.

3. Berry, John. "The Popular Quick Fix, Undermining Library Credibility and Principle." *Library Journal*, (August 1997).

4. California State Education Code, Section 18010.

Special Considerations
for Fee-Based Services
in Academic Libraries

Dorothy D. Smith

SUMMARY. The decision to implement a fee-based service in an academic or public library involves many factors. Research Express, a service at the University of Washington Libraries, started in 1995. The Libraries considered organizing of the service to be necessary to achieve the goal of a user-centered library and included it in strategic planning. This article discusses some of the questions faced in both starting and running Research Express, as well as some general questions for those libraries that might be thinking about setting up a fee-based service. *[Article copies available for a fee from The Haworth Document Delivery Service: 1-800-342-9678. E-mail address: getinfo@haworthpressinc.com <Website: http://www.haworthpressinc.com>]*

KEYWORDS. Fee-based information services, academic libraries, planning, University of Washington Libraries, cost-recovery, value-added

The University of Washington (UW) Libraries opened its fee-based service, Research Express, in fall 1995 after several years of planning. Demand for reference services, online searches, and general informa-

---

Address corespondence to Dorothy D. Smith, Research Express, University of Washington Libraries, Box 352900 Seattle, WA 98195-2900 (Email: dsmith@u.washington.edu).

[Haworth co-indexing entry note]: "Special Considerations for Fee-Based Services in Academic Libraries." Smith, Dorothy D. Co-published simultaneously in *Journal of Interlibrary Loan, Document Delivery & Information Supply* (The Haworth Information Press, an imprint of The Haworth Press, Inc.) Vol. 10, No. 1, 1999, pp. 29-36; and: *Information Delivery in the 21st Century: Proceedings of the Fourth International Conference on Fee-Based Information Services in Libraries* (ed: Suzanne M. Ward, Yem S. Fong, and Tammy Nickelson Dearie) The Haworth Press, Inc., 1999, pp. 29-36. Single or multiple copies of this article are available for a fee from The Haworth Document Delivery Service [1-800-342-9678, 9:00 a.m. - 5:00 p.m. (EST). E-mail address: getinfo@haworthpressinc.com].

tion from non-UW-affiliated users was escalating in a period of staff reductions. At the same time, the addition of CD-ROMs, online databases, and document delivery for campus users left librarians wanting a way to reduce phone calls and reference questions from non-university users. The demand was highest in the libraries specializing in Engineering (also a Patent and Trademark Depository library), Forest Resources, Fisheries-Oceanography, and Business.

As one of the engineering librarians, I was well aware of the need for the service, so I volunteered to get it started. The first step was to define the scope of the service. I believed that the large geographic area we served called for a comprehensive operation similar to those at Michigan, Colorado, Purdue, and Georgia Tech. My suspicion that the initial load would be heavy was soon confirmed, and after the first two months we added another full-time librarian.

Research Express was set up in the largest campus library, Suzzallo, in a former group study room, under the supervision of the Head of Access Services. Access Services reports to the Associate Director for Public Services, and comprises Circulation, Interlibrary Borrowing, Resource Sharing (document delivery), and remote storage. The Libraries agreed to provide start-up costs, but with a goal of the service recovering expenses and salaries as soon as possible.

Here are some of the considerations or decisions involved in setting up such a service, and how they might be different in a public library setting rather than academic.

ACADEMIC VS. PUBLIC

Already Charging

The establishment of a fee-based service at UW was made easier by the fact that the general public is accustomed to paying universities for items such as football tickets, arts events, faculty expertise, and library borrowing privileges or document delivery. Also, in our case, Washington State law prohibits public libraries from charging for services such as online searches, so our public library colleagues were encouraging us to get started.

Database Licenses

Databases, whether CD-ROM, locally loaded, or Web subscriptions, have usage restrictions in the contracts. While public libraries can consider anyone in their geographic area a user, academic libraries are generally prohibited from distributing or using the databases for non-affiliated users. This restriction can make it hard for the fee-based service to convince users to pay for a Dialog search that they could do themselves by coming into the library. There are also questions about whether the databases can be used for citation verification for document delivery.

Technical Expertise

Is there an area in which your librarians are particularly experienced? The ability to do trademark or patentability searches can be a valuable service.

Selling Access

Some fee-based services, such as the PLUS Information Service at the University of California at San Diego, have been successful in getting support from local businesses by putting together a package of services that include library access and parking. Research Express looked at this possibility, but decided we couldn't supply the most valuable piece, the parking!

Contracting

Some fee-based services offer off-site consulting, library services, perhaps cataloging or interlibrary loan, or even library management. Some also outsource research or documents, while others are themselves the recipients of outsourcing by local businesses.

Training

Courses, typically short term, that could be offered by the fee-based service include Web training, library tours, database searching, bibliographic software packages, and anything else which is in demand and that relieves the reference librarians.

Overhead

Will your institution charge you overhead in the form of rent or a surcharge on your fees? Our surcharge is 14.7% and the university takes it from our receipts every quarter. Such a large percentage can make it hard to charge enough for services or to set fees comparable to those charged by the private sector. Heavy surcharges may have been a factor in the demise of some fee-based services.[1]

Distance Learning

Can your fee-based service be involved in planning services for distance learners, or can it provide some of those services? At Research Express, we found that we were helping out distance learners from other universities. We have been involved in discussions at the University of Washington about whether we might provide a referral service or front-end to distance learning questions.

Alumni

Can your alumni continue to get interlibrary borrowing privileges? Do they get a discount for research services? Offering them services through the library's fee-based service might be a way to keep them involved and aware of university resources.

Campus Competition

Are there other fee-based or free library services on campus similar to what you are proposing? Research Express needed to cooperate with Resource Sharing (our longtime document delivery service), as well as with the fee-based service in our health sciences library. The existence of the health sciences service (Health Information for You or HIFY) made it easier to resolve some issues such as pricing, but harder in others, such as competition of customers with overlaps in subject areas. We also needed to consider the services offered by the law school library.

Moonlighting

Are your subject librarians willing or able to do some online searching after hours? If that is not feasible, will they be able to do searches on library time in exchange for extra materials or budget help?

ACADEMIC AND PUBLIC LIBRARIES

There are additional considerations that might be similar for both public and academic institutions.

Demand

What's the demand for extra service in your library? Is it local businesses, science/technology researchers, historians, writers, or remote users? The types of patrons wanting special help can shape the scope of your services, but some types will be better able to pay for them.

Liability

How do you cope with the issues of liability, especially if you do patent, trademark, or any legal searching? What kinds of disclaimers do you need with the information that you provide? In academic libraries, especially state institutions, there is often a legal office or attorney general in place that can help with these questions.

Pricing

Pricing services and documents can be difficult, depending on your competition (inside and outside your own institution) and on your degree of cost recovery necessary. You may inherit prices from previous organizational units. Simple fee structures are the best, but very hard to attain.[2]

ILL

Do you offer interlibrary loan services to the general public or just to your business clients? If you do, how does it fit into the ILL services offered by your library? Should you have separate agreements to avoid compromising the cooperative arrangements you have with other library systems?

Copyright

Do you charge back copyright fees? If so, are they averaged or determined by the document provided? Where do you get the staff to manage the reporting or determining of copyright fees? The University of Washington Libraries does not generally assess copyright, but notifies users of copyright obligations on the material. Research Express does report copyright fees as a service for some businesses.

Ethics

Are there searches or research projects that your service will not perform? How can you tell if you are being asked to do something illegal? Many fee-based services follow the same ethical guidelines as the AIIP (Association of Independent Information Professionals).[3]

Budget

What kind of budget will it take to keep the service subsidized for about three years? The experience with other libraries has shown that this is about how long it takes to get a steady group of customers or to get the service known to patrons.[4] Research Express started with some library endowment funds for salaries, but we used surplus furniture, cast-offs, minimal supplies, and long hours to make it work.

Staff Opposition

What is the general feeling among the librarians and other staff in your library about charging for services? If too many are opposed to it in principle, you may find that you won't get the referrals from public service desks that you need. At the University of Washington some units are able, or consider it their mission, to spend more time serving outside users than others. We suggested that they decide whether to refer based on their workloads or the type of question. As the units learned more about what Research Express can do for patrons, referrals have gone up over the years.

Document Delivery

Is document delivery the main focus of your fee-based service or just part of it? Previous experience seems to suggest that the better your collection, the more you should be able to make from document delivery. Some services fill mostly document delivery orders; others do more research.[5]

Marketing

Can you market your service effectively and do you feel that you can be listed in the Yellow Pages? Marketing is also a continuous challenge if the service is to be able to cover costs. We found that starting with local special librarians was a good strategy, but word-of-mouth and referrals by reference desks has kept us very busy without having to spend much money on marketing.

Competition

Is there opposition to the service in the private sector, especially among information brokers? Research Express was challenged on prices per research hour, but our surcharge on database charges and all out-of-pocket expenses made us more expensive in some instances. At the same time, we made an effort to be reasonably priced for small projects for individuals, because the brokers did not find them cost-effective to handle.

Referrals

How do you promote effective referrals by your reference or information desks? It can be hard to balance giving them enough information to refer patrons correctly, but avoiding the details of prices, delivery times, etc. Research Express offers brown bag sessions, prepares reports, and gives verbal feedback to reference desks about particular queries. We also assure the staff that it was not a problem if only a small percentage of referred patrons eventually agree to a research project.

Staff Expertise

What kind of training is your staff going to need to cope with research requests? Keeping up with online database changes was one problem for reference librarians at Washington, and it contributed to the need for the fee-based service. Do you have particular subjects covered by one researcher or another? The training usually has to be paid for by the fee-based service, and time spent away in training can be costly in terms of billable time lost.

Special Collections

Make good use of those unique collections for which your library is known. If you can link the fee-based service to Web pages or other mentions of those collections, it's also effective marketing. Historical collections or special areas of technical information can be sources for promoting services.

CONCLUSIONS

We consider Research Express a successful fee-based service. Clients continually tell us that we are performing a much-needed service, staff at reference and information desks want us to continue to ease their loads, and we are covering a lot of our costs, maybe soon to be all of them. We hope that we have also contributed to our library's reputation as a major research facility. The long-established fee-based services have served as great role models and were very helpful in our organizational phase. And thanks to Sue Ward for writing the "how-to" book we wish we'd had before, and to Alice Sizer Warner for her excellent guides.

REFERENCES

1. Smith, W. 1993. "Fee-Based Services: Are They Worth It?" *Library Journal* 118(11): p. 42.

2. Warner, A. S. 1989. *Making Money: Fees for Library Services*. New York, NY: Neal-Schuman, p. 65.

3. Association of Independent Information Professionals (AIIP). *http://www.aiip.org*.

4. Drake, M. A. 1997. "Fee-Based Services: the Library's Evolving Enterprise." *MLS: Marketing Library Services* 11(1): p. 3.

5. Ward, S. M. 1997. *Starting and Managing Fee-Based Information Services in Academic Libraries*. Greenwich, CT: JAI Press, p. 24.

Know Your Parent Organization and Your Business Environment– Criteria for Success

Una M. Gourlay

SUMMARY. The culture and structure of each organization are unique. A successful fee-based service will take into account the critical features of its own organization, understanding that strong internal support will be vital for long-term success. Whether the business environment is local, regional, or global, an information provider must understand the overall needs of that environment and be able to satisfy them. Providing services for which costs are not fully recoverable may attract business but be unsustainable in the long run; finding and developing the right niche will build a solid base and lead to long-term success. This paper addresses these issues and identifies strategies for success in both internal and external environments. Since neither environment is static, the issues should be re-examined frequently; since neither environment exists totally independent of the other, it will be beneficial to take advantage of the situations where they overlap or exert influence on each other. *[Article copies available for a fee from The Haworth Document Delivery Service: 1-800-342-9678. E-mail address: getinfo@haworthpressinc.com <Website: http://www.haworthpressinc.com>]*

KEYWORDS. Fee-based information services, organizational culture, business enviroment, cost-recovery, non-profit, policies, planning, marketing, niche services, customer service

---

Una M. Gourlay is Professor Emerita, Fondren Library, Rice University, Houston, Texas.

Address correspondence to Una M. Gourlay, c/o OMS, 1560 West Bay Area Boulevard, Suite 350, Friendswood, TX 77546 (Email: gourlay@rice.edu).

[Haworth co-indexing entry note]: "Know Your Parent Organization and Your Business Environment–Criteria for Success." Gourlay, Una M. Co-published simultaneously in *Journal of Interlibrary Loan, Document Delivery & Information Supply* (The Haworth Information Press, an imprint of The Haworth Press, Inc.) Vol. 10, No. 1, 1999, pp. 37-46; and: *Information Delivery in the 21st Century: Proceedings of the Fourth International Conference on Fee-Based Information Services in Libraries* (ed: Suzanne M. Ward, Yem S. Fong, and Tammy Nickelson Dearie) The Haworth Press, Inc., 1999, pp. 37-46. Single or multiple copies of this article are available for a fee from The Haworth Document Delivery Service [1-800-342-9678, 9:00 a.m. - 5:00 p.m. (EST). E-mail address: getinfo@haworthpressinc.com].

THE PARENT ORGANIZATION

Within its parent organization, a fee-based information service has an external environment–the organization as a whole, and an internal environment–the library or department. A successful fee-based service will take into account the critical features of these environments, with a view to building strong internal support. Begin by learning the culture, policies, and politics of both. Are these cultures entrepreneurial? Is the organization really willing to serve outside clients or is there a sense that it must give primary users a definite priority? Are there actual policies about providing services to people outside the primary constituency? There may be conflict in the attitudes within the organization; for example, regarding lending materials from the library to outside users. While the library community may be comfortable with outside users, there may be strong negative sentiments from the primary users.

What are the politics and conventions regarding particular departments providing external services? For example, is there a tradition that a Continuing Education or an Information Technology Department handles all seminars or training? This is the type of issue that may be raised if you wish to offer training in Web surfing or database searching; or perhaps to provide census information, where the tapes are managed by another department. There might be possible conflicts in providing information services to certain companies or industries that other departments of the organization regard as their particular clients. Be sensitive and aware of what else is happening in the organization; ask many questions and talk to many people. Opposition is sometimes obvious, but not always. Addressing potentially controversial issues by talking to other departments in advance provides the opportunity to form beneficial alliances.

Regardless of the size of the service, you must be aware of the organization's sensitivity to the possibility that you might make a profit. Even if the service is not recovering all costs, there may be a perception within the library, or within the organization as a whole, that you are making money. Administrators of a non-profit organization may be concerned that it will be perceived to be operating a for-profit business. Consult with the attorneys and the controller to ensure that the service is operating within the legally and fiscally sensitive policies of the organization. For a non-profit organization, the issue of unrelated business income should be addressed early. Will the administration be willing to support the service if it seems to be making a profit? At that stage, you can request that they consider the real costs to the library of providing the service. A small positive balance may be considered a justifiable return to the library for hidden costs. Be aware of your state's rules for taxable services, and carefully set up a procedure for collecting and reporting these taxes. Seek advice from the accounting department of the organization regarding retention of satisfactory records for the IRS.

While a strong entrepreneurial spirit is a great asset for successful management of a fee-based service, it is prudent to ensure that the parent organization is comfortable with the scope of the services and the manner in which they are promoted, advertised, and provided. One example is to be aware of legal liability issues and to conform with the organization's requirements if your staff performs online database searches. A second example might be that an opportunity to provide contract staffing or personnel search services must be foregone because these activities will be in conflict with the organization's business mission. Where the service is provided from within a public library, the politics and policies may be defined by a wider organization, such as the city council or an outside board of governors. If the policies are set by elected officers, it may be necessary to present a business plan to, and seek support from, an external group of decision-makers, or even of voters. In some types of non-profit organizations, such as a professional association, the decision-maker may be a board of members or of users. In these situations, successful support will require that you research thoroughly the interests and priorities of the decision-making body.

In some organizations there may be issues concerning what services can be offered for a fee, or whether or not they can be offered to people outside the primary constituency. If the organization is a public library that provides free book loan service and copier service for a small per-page fee on a walk-in basis, will it be permissible for a fee-based service to charge for telephone orders, delivery, on-request photocopying service, and rush processing? Should you be allowed to provide this service to users who are not the library's primary clientele, and if so, should the charges be the same? If the service is being offered by a public institution, will it be viewed as direct or unfair competition to commercial businesses? Having approval from your institution's officers for the manner in which the business is run will increase greatly the likelihood of having real organizational support.

Advice and feedback from people outside the organization can be very helpful. One possibility is to appoint an advisory council; this can be done in different ways, but a successful strategy is to invite senior managers from a variety of types of businesses and possibly add a representative of the senior administration of your own organization. Use the council to keep you informed as to how business is moving and changing its expectations, with respect to the broader issues of information delivery. While this particular model represents mostly influence from the external environment, it can interact positively with the internal environment, such as a university administration, impressing them with the benefits to the organization of providing such a service. You may be instrumental in the formation of alliances between the companies represented and other programs within the institution; thus the fee-based service is credited with contributing to the larger outreach effort of the institution. Such an external group can be an invaluable support for the operation, regardless of the internal environment. It will be most effective if you recruit people who are influential in their own organizations. This strategy has been employed very successfully by R.I.C.E. at Rice University.[1]

THE DEPARTMENT

While the issues that relate to the organization as a whole are important, do not ignore the immediate environment, the library or its equivalent. Expect that there may be some internal opposition or resentment to the fee-based operation, whether it is set up separately from the other services, with totally separate staff, or whether it is run from within a department, such as reference or interlibrary loan. Other staff may feel that it is not appropriate to have such a service; they may think that the materials should be available only for primary users or that the service and its staff are getting extra privileges, benefits, or attention. This resentment may not be obvious, but you should watch for clues, get feedback from supportive staff, and address the issues promptly. All staff should understand what the service does and that it has administrative support; they should be given explanations for any special treatment necessary to make the service successful. Demonstrate that the service benefits the library or department as a whole.

Even a service that is only recovering costs can give something back to the library. For example, if the service has available money, buy some extra equipment that other departments can use. If that is not possible, perhaps your staff can show support to other departments by offering help in emergencies, managing the courier services for the whole library, or providing a table of contents service for staff.

An established service can run into unexpected difficulties if the library administration changes or if there is a drastic cut in budgets. The administration may threaten to close down the service if it is seen as taking resources away from other operations, or if there is a change in priorities regarding services for primary users. Counteracting these arguments may be difficult; to be successful, your strategy must address the particular issues. One solution is to develop more services for the library's primary clientele. If the staff works exclusively in the fee-based department, it might be beneficial to integrate them with other staff; by doing so you must demonstrate that you can provide a better service for all users. This could be effected by having a combined staff for document delivery and interlibrary loan, or for research services, to both campus and business clients. If your staff is already integrated, the effective strategy may be to separate them, then to provide financial proof that the operation is recovering all costs, and that it is not a drain on the library or department resources. Finding the right solution will depend on the particular situation and will require ingenuity, but if you feel strongly about preserving the service, such drastic changes will be worthwhile. You may be able to show, by a creative presentation of the statistics, that the service already has provided some financial support for the library, for example, by underwriting some of the costs of another unit, such as interlibrary loan. Perhaps you can demonstrate that the outreach effort of the service has brought back benefits to the library or to the organization; by recognition from the community; by bringing in support for other operations, such as donations of equipment; or by increased membership in a friends' organization. In fact, even when things are going well, this type of report is valuable, since it boosts the image of the service within the library and may catch the attention of the senior administration.

Recognition within the institution can be elusive, even for an established service. One solution is to mark an anniversary or other special event by holding a reception for clients, senior administrators, deans, and other notable people from the library and business community. Such an event should merit good publicity within the organization; with invited guests representing an impressive and diverse array of interests, the service will gain valuable internal recognition and the library or supporting department will receive positive attention.

You will effectively demonstrate the common needs of the internal and external communities if you provide services to the organization's primary users. For example, some departments may require unusual information services for special projects; perhaps there are grant funds available to pay for in-depth research, statistics gathering, prior art, or marketability studies. You should never miss an opportunity to promote the service internally, since high profile support within the organization is always useful. While these last ideas seem to relate more to the organization as a whole, in fact they are powerful arguments to the library administration that the service is a valuable asset.

THE BUSINESS ENVIRONMENT

A fee-based service must find the right niche in its business environment; when you establish a new service, you should identify and target the most obvious market. Develop the services that will serve that base market and become proficient in providing these services before you move on to seek a broader client base. The exact nature of your established base will depend on geographic location, demographic distribution in the immediate area, types of local businesses, existing competition or other information facilities available, and other factors. Recognize that different types of businesses have individual characteristics regarding the quantity of external information they use and the amount of money they are prepared to spend. If your primary market is composed of large companies, the range of services required may be very different than if it is dominated by small businesses. Investigate the profiles and patterns of the local business environment; this research will aid your development of an effective business plan. You may have the good fortune to find some companies in your business community that value information highly and understand its cost. Work diligently to get their business; find out what they need and how they wish to have it delivered; do as much as possible for them. They will provide you with a significant income and the comfort of some financial security. You will be able to make a much greater margin for value-added services than for basic document delivery and database searching. Examples are to analyze statistics, summarize research output, or other forms of post-processing. However this work is only good business if the client is willing to pay well for the professional time involved. There are also some types of services that bring better returns for outlay of manpower than others. One example is a service provided by FYI at Los Angeles County Library[2] where staff compile standard packages of company and business profiles that can be delivered repeatedly. In a tight market, where there is keen competition, or where companies have not been accustomed to paying for information, being seen to give value for money is most important. In that type of market it is much harder to make good margins. Even a small positive margin can be worthwhile if the volume of the service provided is significant, but be vigilant to ensure that costs do not exceed income.

Thorough investigation of the local business environment may uncover creative opportunities for some guaranteed income. For example, if you are in a state that provides assistance for small businesses, you may be able to contract with your state or local government to give information services at a discounted rate. The Technical Information Service (TIS) at Purdue University[3] started in this way, then later developed a significant clientele of larger businesses. An assured income is a valuable base on which to build. You may find benefits if you can make your internal and external environments work together. One way to accomplish this is to contract with a program in your organization to give information services to their clients; successful examples are PLUS at UCSD[4] and Corporate and Research Services at Georgia Tech[5] which provide information services for their institutions' corporate sponsors programs. You may have to create the opportunity by approaching the individual research sponsorship programs in your organization with the suggestion that they offer information services to their members, either as a package or at a discounted rate.

Know your local business environment well enough to be aware of any legal or cultural issues that may prevent a fee-based service from succeeding. For example, if you belong to a state institution, determine if there are state laws that pertain to competition with the commercial sector. If this is likely to be an issue, you should consider offering services that are not in direct competition. Become ac-

quainted with the local information providers and seek to work coop-
eratively with them. Perhaps you can refer clients and give business to
each other. Develop a friendly relationship; work together with them
in local information associations; or collaborate in community outreach projects.

As you develop your primary market, determine the manner in
which your clients wish to conduct their business with you. Do they
like to communicate with you by Email and a Web page, or are they
more comfortable talking to a person or sending a fax? Do they want
to develop a real relationship (usually a good situation) or do they
prefer to see you simply as a vendor, providing a product, with minimum interaction? Your staffing and equipment levels must reflect the
needs of your primary users; be equipped to meet their requirements
for quality and timeliness, and their expectations for communication
and delivery. Develop real relationships with your clients and you will
build client loyalty. Find ways to get to know each other. If they are
distant or very busy, perhaps an electronic newsletter with opportunities for interaction will be their style. If they like a more personal
approach, call them up once in a while; invite them to a coffee or a
seminar. Give all your clients frequent opportunities for feedback.
Seek good publicity so that your clients see you as a local fixture; be
active in sponsoring local events, in both library circles and the community at large. Such efforts will encourage your existing clients to
use your services, and most definitely will attract more business.

For public libraries there is the sensitive issue of whether or not
clients may be charged. In this situation, by taking care to learn about
your local environment, you will be able to choose the services for
which the clients are willing to pay. In general, you will be most
successful if you provide services that you can do better or faster than
they can themselves. Do not overlook the peculiarities and special
opportunities of your market. An example is the success of FYI at LA
County Library[2] that caters very effectively to the special needs of
businesses related to the entertainment industry.

When you have reached the point that you are serving your primary
market well, and you begin to reach out beyond it, the issues related to
excellence of service become harder to address. Acquisition of clients
in different types of business or at more remote locations presents new
challenges in terms of communications and delivery. The Internet is an
alluring opportunity for more casual business, but explore it cautious-

ly; be sure that you are ready for that type of market. No fee-based service has just one homogeneous market, even at the local level. You may have one or two strong core markets, but certainly you will have peripheral business. If you break into a new market, you must determine that it is worthwhile and that you can make money or recover costs. You may be prepared to make a smaller margin than usual, or even an initial loss, to get a foothold in a high profile market, but take care. Be prepared to walk away if you think you have made a mistake. If you find that you have over-extended your capabilities, restrict the services you offer to those with which you are most comfortable. There are many reasons why you might choose not to stay in a new market. One might be that you don't have enough of the materials or resources that the clients need; therefore, you have to fill their orders from secondary sources, making your service appear slow or expensive. Perhaps you must hire additional specialized staff and you cannot recover all the added expense. A third reason might be that the clients require a faster turnaround than you can consistently provide.

FINAL THOUGHTS

You will serve your clients best and have the highest user satisfaction if you provide services with which you are comfortable. Bigger and more are not always better. Reach an agreement with your administration regarding the nature and quantity of the services you will provide. Provide services that have the endorsement of your organization; that satisfy the information needs of your clients; and that you can deliver consistently with excellence.

Your parent organization and your business environment together will determine your fate; if you do not take time to know and understand them, your fee-based service may not last. By working with them creatively and sensitively, you will have the potential for a successful operation.

REFERENCES

1. Regional Information & Communication Exchange (R.I.C.E.), Fondren Library, Rice University, Houston, Texas: Damon Camille, Director.

2. FYI, Los Angeles County Library, Los Angeles, California; Steve Coffman, Director.

   3. Technical Information Service (TIS), Purdue University Libraries, West Lafayette, Indiana; Suzanne Ward, Head, Access Services.

   4. PLUS, University of California, San Diego, Social Sciences & Humanities Library, La Jolla, California: Tammy Nickelson Dearie, Director, Access & Delivery Services.

   5. Corporate Research Services, Georgia Institute of Technology, Library, Atlanta, Georgia: Katharine Calhoun, Director.

Writing an Effective Business Plan for Fee-Based Services

Pamela J. MacKintosh

SUMMARY. This paper addresses the basics of writing a business plan. Although some literature on fee-based library services and information brokering mentions business plans, most of the material on this topic can be found in the traditional business literature. Therefore, business literature will create the framework for this paper, but has been modified to better describe operations of fee-based library services when they differ from for-profit businesses. *[Article copies available for a fee from The Haworth Document Delivery Service: 1-800-342-9678. E-mail address: getinfo@haworthpressinc.com <Website: http://www.haworthpressinc.com>]*

KEYWORDS. Fee-based information services, marketing, business plans, planning, market analysis, budgets, non-profit

WHAT IS A BUSINESS PLAN?

There are many definitions of a business plan. The Small Business Administration Web page states, "A business plan precisely defines

Pamela J. MacKintosh is Senior Associate Librarian and Head, Michigan Information Transfer Source (MITS), University Library, University of Michigan.

Address correspondence to Pamela J. MacKintosh, MITS, University of Michigan, 100 Hatcher Graduate Library, 920 North University Avenue, Ann Arbor, MI 48109-1205.

[Haworth co-indexing entry note]: "Writing an Effective Business Plan for Fee-Based Services." MacKintosh, Pamela J. Co-published simultaneously in *Journal of Interlibrary Loan, Document Delivery & Information Supply* (The Haworth Information Press, an imprint of The Haworth Press, Inc.) Vol. 10, No. 1, 1999, pp. 47-61; and: *Information Delivery in the 21st Century: Proceedings of the Fourth International Conference on Fee-Based Information Services in Libraries* (ed: Suzanne M. Ward, Yem S. Fong, and Tammy Nickelson Dearie) The Haworth Press, Inc., 1999, pp. 47-61. Single or multiple copies of this article are available for a fee from The Haworth Document Delivery Service [1-800-342-9678, 9:00 a.m. - 5:00 p.m. (EST). E-mail address: getinfo@haworthpressinc.com].

your business, identifies your goals and serves as your firm's resume.
. . . It helps you allocate resources properly, handle unforeseen com-
plications, and make the right decisions."[1] In *How to Write a Successful Business Plan*, Julie Brooks and Barry Stevens describe the business plan as "a process you undertake to help make your company
grow, to increase profits, or to develop and market a product idea or
service."[2] Some fee-based services' managers may think that business
plans are not necessary since we typically run non-profit, cost-recovery organizations within public or academic libraries, instead of for-
profit businesses. Despite the fact that we generally don't apply for
bank loans or try to make a profit, there are still reasons for preparing
a business plan. Fee-based services' plans may just need to be focused
toward a different audience or purpose. David Gumpert addresses this
point in his book on business plans. According to Gumpert, "The
planning process is much the same for non-profit and government
organizations as for business. These organizations need to develop a
strategy, target their markets, focus on product and/or service quality,
and attend to all the other matters that a business must consider. But in
addition to business considerations, nonbusiness organizations must
pay attention to an additional factor: their governing constituencies. . . .
The members of these governing bodies may have different agendas
and interests than the executives running the organizations on a day-
to-day basis."[3] The statement about governing bodies is particularly
true for fee-based services in libraries. Often the library director or
board may have goals for the service that go beyond those of providing information services, such as generating revenue for other parts of
the library or serving a public relations function for the library. As a
final definition for business plans, Gumpert nicely sums it up as, "A
successful business plan is one that focuses your thinking, helps you
establish a realistic business strategy, improves your operations, and
wins for your company the financing and other support it needs."[4]

WHY WRITE A BUSINESS PLAN?

Business plans can serve a variety of purposes. They are written for
many different reasons and are targeted to different audiences. Some
reasons for writing a business plan include asking for a bank loan,
seeking investors, attracting clients, bidding on a project, and gaining
permission from a library director or board to start a fee-based service.

In addition to reaching external audiences, business plans can also address internal audiences and purposes. A business plan can be prepared to ensure that the unit's staff understands the goals and focus of the service. Finally, and perhaps most importantly, writing a business plan will help the service manager focus his thinking regarding the unit and how it should be managed. According to Gregory Massarella, Patrick Zorsch, Daniel Jacobson, and Marc Rittenhouse, one of the plan's key benefits to internal users is "heightened motivation and learning resulting from involvement in the planning process, including a more complete understanding of the business premise and economics"[5]. Thus the business plan can be a very valuable management tool for the fee-based service manager.

Although most business plans cover the same basic content, the major thrust of the plan will vary based on its purpose. If the plan's main purpose is to seek funding for the fee-based service, then it will focus on the predictability of cash flow, debt coverage, the financial management expertise of the manager, the percent of investment by the owner (i.e., the risk she is willing to take), the scope of the market, and the profit potential of the company. A plan primarily intended to aid in internal planning and management of the organization should emphasize clear communication of the business concept and strategy, how this operation fits into the rest of the organization's goals, contingency plans, strengths and weaknesses of the organization, and a baseline against which to measure the unit's progress in meeting its goals.

WHAT GOES IN A BUSINESS PLAN?

As mentioned above, although the contents and focus of a business plan will vary somewhat based on its intended purpose and audience, for the most part a business plan contains the following: cover page, table of contents, executive summary, company overview, market analysis, competitor analysis, products and/or services offered, marketing, sales, and promotion strategies, information on the organization's management team, and financials. In the next few paragraphs, each of these sections will be described in greater detail. Some areas included in a typical business plan, such as sections on manufacturing capabilities, complex distribution systems, or detailed production information are unnecessary in a plan for a fee-based information service.

THE BUSINESS PLAN STEP-BY-STEP

Cover Page

The cover page should include enough information to identify the organization and the contact person. This point is particularly important if the document is going to an external audience, such as a bank loan officer. The cover page typically includes the name of the company, its address (both the street and mailing address, if different, would be important if the audience is external to the service's parent organization), its telephone and fax numbers as well as its Web address, the contact name (usually the president or CEO, though in the case of a library fee-based service, the service manager or the library administrator proposing the service), and the date.

Table of Contents

A table of contents follows the cover page. The point at which the table of contents is created is one of the few areas in which the experts disagree. Some of the literature suggests that the table of contents be written first and used as an outline to ensure that all necessary sections are included in the plan. Other authors indicate that the table of contents should be prepared after the plan is finished. In either case, it should be complete and include page numbers for the beginning of each section.

Executive Summary

Next comes the executive summary. This section should be two to three pages long and present the plan in miniature. It should set the priorities for the service. Since the executive summary is often the only chance a service or new business is given to spark the interest of the decision-makers, it should be written to capture the reader's attention. The fee-based service should be defined in non-library jargon. Indicate the rationale for starting the service and explain the benefits to the library (or parent organization or funding source, as the case may be). The executive summary should include the fee-based service's mission statement, as well as a description of the products and services offered. The summary outlines requirements for staff, equipment, space, and other necessities. It should also include basic marketing ideas and budget highlights. Information on the initial funding sources (loan, government subsidy, grant funds) should be given, as well as an estimate on how long it will take for the service to be self-sufficient and able to repay outstanding loans. The summary should also include an implementation timeline outlining when the new service will be launched. According to Suzanne Ward in her book *Starting and Managing Fee-Based Information Services in Academic Libraries*, the manager should "[w]rite the summary so that it can stand on its own. The library director may use the summary alone to acquaint university administrators with the proposal."[6] Each of the areas addressed in the summary will be expanded upon in greater detail in the body of the business plan.

Company Overview

After the executive summary, the plan should include a company overview. This section provides the basic information on the company or service. It includes the company's business strategy, mission statement, current status, objectives and goals, and major successes or achievements to date. According to Gumpert, this is the section "where you spell out your company's philosophy and logic–its reason for being, its identity."[7]

Market Analysis

A key section of the business plan is the market analysis. In this section, the business plan author must answer or address several questions: What is your market? Who are the potential customers? What is the size of the market, and what portion of it can you reasonably hope to get? How much of the product or service will each customer buy? These questions need to be answered as specifically as possible. For example, in identifying potential customers, it is not really useful to say "anyone who is willing to pay for our services" or "businesses in our state." The business plan audience, the person or people who will decide whether the service is allowed to be established or to get additional funding, will want details on specific markets. For example, indicate whether the service will target medium-sized law firms within the service's metropolitan area, or engineers in research and development-oriented companies in the tri-state area. If the service is partially funded by state economic development funds, then the service may need to focus on new businesses or industries moving into the state or those going through restructuring. Another way to define clients is geographically. In a large metropolitan area, the service can focus on local business; for those in less populated regions, the client net may need to be thrown out farther. Will in-state clients or university donors be considered primary clientele, or will the service seek clients nationwide or around the world? For existing services, this focused look at the market can be based on current and past experience with key users of your service. For those who are writing a plan for a proposed service, usually there has been some external demand for services that has triggered the decision to consider a fee-based service. Indicate who has been asking for services, but also think about whether they would really become paying customers should the service be created. It is also important to look at how much of a product or service will be purchased and what client groups would be repeat customers. Private individuals may request an article or a literature search, but they rarely become large revenue-generating, repeat customers. They usually come for one specific need. Business clients, lawyers, and consultants, on the other hand, are more likely to become repeat customers. They will have both ongoing information needs and the financial resources to pay for services on a regular basis. The business plan writer needs to determine what products or services she can reasonably expect to sell and how much of each she can expect each client to buy. In his book *How to Develop a Business Plan in 15 Days*, William Luther says that "the target audience, sometimes referred to as heavy users, comprises the 20 percent of the individuals or companies in the marketplace that should account for at least 80 percent of your profit."[8]

To do market research the fee-based service manager will need to call upon his or her reference skills. Since most fee-based services managers have past experience as reference librarians, this article will not go into detail on how to find relevant market information, but the business plan writer should look at government statistics, trade literature, business directories, and market analyst reports in preparing the business plan's market analysis section.

Competitor Analysis

In addition to looking at the potential market, the business plan should also include a section that evaluates the competition. In this section, the fee-based service manager will need to answer the following questions: Who else is selling the service or product you sell? Who else can meet the market's need (even if not with similar products or services)? What are your competitors' strengths and weaknesses? According to Gumpert, you need to "explain what the company will do to exceed and stay ahead of the competition"[9] In looking at the competition, the fee-based service manager needs to consider a wide range of possibilities. Although the obvious competitors would be local independent information brokers and the potential clients' corporate libraries, other competitors could include business consultants, the public library, the Internet, the clients' co-workers, book stores, and the clients' lack of understanding that they even need the type of services we can provide.

Products and Services Offered

After evaluating the competition, the business plan outlines what products or services will be offered in the market. This section includes a description of what the product/service is and what it does. The plan should explain how the products/services meet the market needs, outline specific benefits to customers, and include pricing information. Pricing can be particularly problematic for librarians who are used to providing free services. First, the manager will need to figure out all of the costs (both direct and indirect), and then set prices to cover all of the costs. The manager will need to determine if there will be differential pricing (will clients who commit funds up front, through a subscription plan or deposit account, receive a discount?). If the service is funded partially by a state grant, then in-state clients may need to be charged a rate that is lower than that for out-of-state clients. Production issues need to be addressed. Although this is typically more important in a manufacturing industry, service organizations still need to determine if their products/services can be produced in a timely manner, consistently, and cost effectively. According to Gumpert, "The market and what it values should determine the particulars of the products or services"[10.] After all, just because we can produce something of high quality on a consistent basis does not mean anyone will have a need for it or want to pay the price to buy.

Marketing Strategy

The next section of the business plan covers the marketing strategy. According to Gumpert, "The marketing section of your business plan should be focused on the *benefits* rather than on the *features* of your company's product or service."[11] The marketing strategy should include specific information on how the fee-based service will market its products and services. The strategy will vary based on the specific services and the potential market, but could include such activities as sales calls, direct mail, a booth at trade shows, and talks at business clubs. The plan should also outline how the service will promote interest in its products and services. Promotional examples include advertising, press releases, brochures, Web pages, and referrals by other library units.

The marketing strategy section should also set goals for marketing. This includes identifying how to evaluate if the marketing has been successful and how to know which marketing activities to try again and which to drop. Part of this evaluation mechanism should include determining who are the service's key customers and why they use the service, evaluating what services or products these key customers have purchased, determining what their purchasing levels are, and determining how purchases are affected by price, turnaround time, quality, and other measures.

Management

The management section of the business plan describes the management team. Unlike big companies, the fee-base service does not usually have a "management team." The service may start with just the manager and perhaps some student assistants. This section should include information on the service manager (and any other key staff) such as his resume, relevant experience, educational background, strengths in relation to the fee-based service's operations, and real life accomplishments that could have a bearing on the success of the service. It is important to make sure that all key business areas are covered (management, financial/accounting, research, and sales/marketing). It is unlikely that any one fee-based service manager will have expertise and experience in all of these areas, especially in the early years. In that case explain who will provide the needed expertise. The service may need to hire outside consultants, such as a graphic designer and professional writer to prepare the brochures and newsletter. The fee-based unit may call upon the services of others within the parent organization, for example hiring the library's business office to do the billing or the campus public relations office to help with marketing. Often in academic environments the service can hire (or have as a class project or practicum experience) a business school student to help with marketing or questionnaire design, a library science student to help with document retrieval or OCLC searching, or an art student to design a logo or the graphics for the unit Web page. It is important, though, to remember that students come and go and may not be committed beyond a course grade. It may be more cost effective in the long run to hire a real consultant or permanent staff than to depend on the assistance of students.

Financial Analysis

The final required section of the business plan is the financial analysis. Alice Sizer Warner states, "The financial plan shows your best, realistic estimates of the future for your business."[12] This section should include a five-year financial estimate, with the first two years providing monthly figures and the last three years in quarterly figures. The financial estimates should include a cash flow statement (Figure 1), an income (or profit and loss) statement (Figure 2), and a balance sheet (Figure 3). They should follow generally accepted accounting procedures. This format will make it easier to compare the service's numbers with those generated by the university's financial office and will make the service's records more persuasive should the unit ever be audited. The actual line items will vary from service to service. Samples of these financial statements can be found in most accounting texts. Although the budget estimates are essential if you are applying for a bank loan or other outside funding, it is important even if the plan is just going to the library administration. The library director will want a realistic estimate of when the unit will become self-sustaining.

Clarifying whether a service has a realistic chance of becoming cost-recovery is also an important point in those plans that are being used to determine if a new service should be launched. Some organizations are not concerned about whether the fee-based service becomes self-sufficient. But even in this situation, the administration will still need an estimate of what the information service will cost the organization in way of annual subsidies. If the library expects the service to generate additional funds to support other library functions, the director will want an estimate of when she can expect to see those revenue streams flowing into the library.

Appendix

The last section in the business plan is the appendix (or appendices, if need be). The appendix might include a copy of the service's brochure, a price list, product samples, or other things the manager wants to share with the business plan reader.

BUSINESS PLAN CONSULTANTS

Some readers may wonder if it is really prudent to write a business plan oneself, when a business plan consultant could be hired to do this. Although this may seem like a good idea, hiring an expert has some major drawbacks. First, the consultant will not understand the business as well as the manager. This is especially true for a fee-based service, since this type of operation is often a complete novelty to those outside the library world. Second, if a consultant prepares the plan, the service manager may not know the contents of the plan well enough to answer detailed questions about it when questioned by the library director or other plan audience. Finally, since the plan is a guide to managing the business, the manager should not abdicate the responsibility of creating this very useful management and planning tool.

BUSINESS PLAN SOFTWARE

Instead of writing a plan from scratch, one can use business plan software to guide the process. Although software prompts the writer

FIGURE 1. Cash Flow Statement

Company Name				
Monthly Cash Flow Statement 199_ -199_ ($000)				
	January	February	March	April
Beginning Cash Balance				
Receipts				
Collection of receivables				
Savings				
Interest income				
Other				
Total Cash Receipts				
Cash Disbursements				
Salaries				
Fringe benefits				
Accounts payable				
Supplies				
Rent				
Equipment				
Advertising				
Taxes				
Loan payments				
Online database fees				
Copy cards				
Royalty/copyright fees				
Training				
Other				
Total Disbursements				
Ending Cash Balance/Cash on Hand				

through the process and reduces the chance of leaving out an important section, there are disadvantages. First, the software is a canned program. Typically, all plans produced from a software package will look and "feel" alike. If the plan's audience sees a lot of business plans, as in the case of the bank loan officer, this lack of uniqueness could be a problem. In addition, using software could limit the chance for creativity. The plan writer may be forced to stick to a prescribed format. This limitation could be a real problem for a fee-based service, since it is different in nature than a for-profit business. Although the products discussed have probably been superceded by now, Hertz and

FIGURE 2. Income Statement (Profit and Loss Statement)

Company Name				
Quarterly Income Statement 199_ – 199_ ($000)				
	1st Qt	2nd Qt	3rd Qt	4th Qt
(a) Sales Revenue				
(b) Cost of Goods Sold				
(b1) Direct labor				
(b2) Materials				
(c) Gross Profit [a-(b1+b2)]				
(d) Expenses				
(d1) Salaries				
(d2) Marketing				
(d3) Supplies				
(d4) Depreciation				
(d5) Taxes				
(d6) Other expenses				
(e) Total Expenses (d1+d2, etc.)				
(f) Net profIt/loss (c-e)				

McWilliams give details on business plan software features and how to evaluate them.

REALITY CHECK

Now for a few caveats and a reality check. To do a full-blown business plan, complete with all of the market research and competitor analysis, could take a team of experts weeks to perhaps several months to prepare. Most fee-based services are understaffed, often with only one permanent staff member. Fee-based services do not typically have the excess capacity to pull anyone off his or her regular duties to devote weeks to doing the research needed to write a comprehensive plan. This is especially true for an existing service that is writing a plan as an ongoing management tool. If the library is in the early stages of creating a service, someone has probably been given a block of time to explore these issues carefully. If, however, the manager of a nascent service is writing a plan, she will need to build the time required to research and write the plan into the estimates for the time

FIGURE 3. Balance Sheet

Company Name				
Quarterly Balance Sheet 199_ –199_ ($000)				
	1st Qt	2nd Qt	3rd Qt	4th Qt
Assets				
Cash				
Accounts receivable				
Deposit accounts/prepaid expenses				
Equipment				
Less accumulated depreciation				
Other				
Total assets				
Liabilities				
Accounts payable				
Taxes payable				
Outstanding loans/notes payable				
Unearned income				
Other liabilities				
Total Liabilities				
Equity				
Total Liabilities and Equity				

required to break even. Time spent planning is time that cannot be spent doing billable work. An informal survey among FISCAL (Fee-Based Information Service Centers in Academic Libraries) members and a few independent information brokers revealed that very few information service managers have prepared a complete business plan. Despite this, most agree it is important to plan. Finding time to write the plan often means doing individual parts of it at different times. Perhaps the financial analysis is done during the annual budget cycle, and the product and service review may be done later to determine if a new service should be added or a weak service dropped. Even just doing pieces of the plan can be very valuable to the fee-based service manager, as it requires the manager to evaluate the service, to think about what is working and what is not, and to come up with strategies to make improvements.

NOTES

1. Small Business Administration. *The Business Plan Road Map to Success: A Tutorial and Self-paced Activity.* Modified Sep. 1997: http://www.sbaonline.sba.gov/ starting/businessplan.html

2. Brooks, Julie K. and Barry A. Stevens. *How to Write a Successful Business Plan.* New York: AMACOM, 1987. p.2.

3. Gumpert, David E. *Inc. Magazine Presents How to Really Create a Successful Business Plan: Featuring the Business Plans of Pizza Hut, Software Publishing Corp., Celestial Seasonings, People Express, Ben & Jerry's.* Rev. and expanded 3rd ed. Boston: Inc. Publishing, 1996. p. 18-19.

4. Gumpert, David E. *Inc. Magazine Presents How to Really Create a Successful Business Plan: Featuring the Business Plans of Pizza Hut, Software Publishing Corp., Celestial Seasonings, People Express, Ben & Jerry's.* Rev. and expanded 3rd ed. Boston: Inc. Publishing, 1996. p. 4.

5. Massarella, Gregory J., Patrick D. Zorsch, Daniel D. Jacobson, and Marc J. Ritenhouse. *How to Prepare a Results-Driven Business Plan.* New York: AMACOM, 1993. p. 12.

6. Ward, Suzanne M. *Starting and Managing Fee-Based Information Services in Academic Libraries.* Greenwich, CT.: JAI Press, Inc., 1997. p. 74.

7. Gumpert, David E. *Inc. Magazine Presents How to Really Create a Successful Business Plan: Featuring the Business Plans of Pizza Hut, Software Publishing Corp., Celestial Seasonings, People Express, Ben & Jerry's.* Rev. and expanded 3rd ed. Boston: Inc. Publishing, 1996. p. 73.

8. Luther, William H. *How to Develop a Business Plan in 15 Days.* New York: AMACOM, 1987. p. 49.

9. Gumpert, David E. *Inc. Magazine Presents How to Really Create a Successful Business Plan: Featuring the Business Plans of Pizza Hut, Software Publishing Corp., Celestial Seasonings, People Express, Ben & Jerry's.* Rev. and expanded 3rd ed. Boston: Inc. Publishing, 1996. p. 103.

10. Gumpert, David E. *Inc. Magazine Presents How to Really Create a Successful Business Plan: Featuring the Business Plans of Pizza Hut, Software Publishing Corp., Celestial Seasonings, People Express, Ben & Jerry's.* Rev. and expanded 3rd ed. Boston: Inc. Publishing, 1996. p. 112.

11. Gumpert, David E. *Inc. Magazine Presents How to Really Create a Successful Business Plan: Featuring the Business Plans of Pizza Hut, Software Publishing Corp., Celestial Seasonings, People Express, Ben & Jerry's.* Rev. and expanded 3rd ed.. Boston: Inc. Publishing, 1996. p. 97.

12. Warner, Alice Sizer. *Mind Your Own Business: A Guide for the Information Entrepreneur.* New York: Neal-Schuman, 1987. p. 36.

REFERENCES

Baechler, Mary. "Do Business Plans Matter?" *Inc.* Feb. 1996: 21.

Brooks, Julie K. and Barry A. Stevens. *How to Write a Successful Business Plan.* New York: AMACOM, 1987.

Brokaw, Leslie. "The Business Plan: Dream v. Reality." *Executive Female.* Mar.-Apr. 1996: 60+.

Brown, Carolyn M. "The Do's and Don'ts of Writing a Winning Business Plan." *Black Enterprise.* Apr. 1996: 114+.

Elkins, Linda. "Tips for Preparing a Business Plan." *Nation's Business.* June 1996: 60R-61R.

Gumpert, David E. *Inc. Magazine Presents How to Really Create a Successful Business Plan: Featuring the Business Plans of Pizza Hut, Software Publishing Corp., Celestial Seasonings, People Express, Ben & Jerry's.* Rev. and expanded 3rd ed.. Boston: Inc. Publishing, 1996.

Hertz, Frank. "Focus Your Goals." *Success.* Sep. 1996: 60-64.

Levinson, Jay Conrad. "Plan of Attack." *Inc.* Jan. 1997: 84-85.

Luther, William H. *How to Develop a Business Plan in 15 Days.* New York: AMACOM, 1987.

Mancuso, Joseph R. *How to Prepare and Present a Business Plan.* Englewood Cliffs, N.J.: Prentice-Hall, 1983.

Massarella, Gregory J., Patrick D. Zorsch, Daniel D. Jacobson, and Marc J. Ritenhouse. *How to Prepare a Results-Driven Business Plan.* New York: AMACOM, 1993.

McLaughlin, Harold J. *Building Your Business Plan: A Step by-Step Approach.* New York: John Wiley & Sons, 1985.

McWilliams, Brian. "Garbage in, Garbage out." *Inc.* Aug. 1996: 41-44.

Ojala, Marydee. "Business Plans for Small Businesses." *Database.* Aug.-Sep. 1995: 78-80.

Small Business Administration. *The Business Plan Road Map to Success: A Tutorial and Self-Paced Activity.* Modified Sep. 1997: http://www.sbaonline.sba.gov/ starting/businessplan.html

Stevens, Mark. "Seven Steps to a Well-Prepared Business Plan." *Executive Female.* Mar.-Apr. 1995: 30-31.

Ward, Suzanne M. *Starting and Managing Fee-Based Information Services in Academic Libraries.* Greenwich, Ct.: JAI Press, Inc., 1997.

Warner, Alice Sizer. *Making Money: Fees for Library Services.* New York: Neal-Schuman, [1989?].

Warner, Alice Sizer. *Mind Your Own Business: A Guide for the Information Entrepreneur.* New York: Neal-Schuman, 1987.

Wichman, William. "Mapping out Effective Annual Business Plans." *Bank Marketing.* Nov. 1995: 48-52.

Pricing and Costing in Fee-Based Information Services

Yem S. Fong

SUMMARY. Setting prices in fee-based information services presents many challenges. Each service and its parent institution have a different definition of "cost recovery" and a different set of local accounting rules and procedures. The manager assesses the organizational goals and strategies, and then reviews the standard pricing models to determine which one best matches local objectives. This paper explores cost accounting methodology to illustrate one method of costing services and determining prices to cover those costs. *[Article copies available for a fee from The Haworth Document Delivery Service: 1-800-342-9678. E-mail address: getinfo@haworthpressinc.com <Website: http://www.haworthpressinc.com>]*

KEYWORDS. Fee-based information services, planning, budgets, pricing, non-profit, cost-recovery, cost accounting goals, value-added, University of Colorado at Boulder Libraries

Fee-based information services in libraries typically operate on principles of cost recovery. A simple statement, but what exactly does "cost recovery" mean? The obvious answer is that it means different things to different types of organizations. From publicly supported to

Yem S. Fong is Associate Professor and Head, Information Delivery Services, University of Colorado at Boulder, Campus Box 184, Boulder, CO 80309 (fongj@spot.colorado.edu).

[Haworth co-indexing entry note]: "Pricing and Costing in Fee-Based Information Services." Fong, Yem S. Co-published simultaneously in *Journal of Interlibrary Loan, Document Delivery & Information Supply* (The Haworth Information Press, an imprint of The Haworth Press, Inc.) Vol. 10, No. 1, 1999, pp. 63-73; and: *Information Delivery in the 21st Century: Proceedings of the Fourth International Conference on Fee-Based Information Services in Libraries* (ed: Suzanne M. Ward, Yem S. Fong, and Tammy Nickelson Dearie) The Haworth Press, Inc., 1999, pp. 63-73. Single or multiple copies of this article are available for a fee from The Haworth Document Delivery Service [1-800-342-9678, 9:00 a.m. - 5:00 p.m. (EST). E-mail address: getinfo@haworth.pressinc. com].

well funded special libraries, the expectations and realities of cost recovery vary greatly. No matter what the organizational structure, these services ultimately face the bottom line of charging fees for value added services.

The mandate for most fee-based information services is to be self-supporting, either partially or fully. They are expected to generate enough revenue to cover staff salaries and benefits, capital equipment costs, supplies, and other operational overhead. Some libraries support the salaries and benefits of staff in fee-based services hoping to charge enough to cover out-of-pocket expenses. At the other end of the spectrum are institutions that require the fee-based service to recover 100% of its costs, plus pay a substantial overhead fee to the library or the campus. In a third model, a library's fee-for-service unit shares offices, staffing, and space within a larger or combined department. In this model costs and expenses may be shared with the expectation that revenue or staffing from the fee-based unit goes to supporting the larger department, or that library funded resources support the fee-based service.

How do these departments charge for document delivery and research services? What criteria can be used to set fees? Managers of fee-based units have developed numerous strategies to identify expenses and to determine prices. Based on experiences at the University of Colorado Technical Research Center (CTRC), this paper highlights pricing scenarios and cost accounting methodology for setting prices.

ORGANIZATIONAL GOALS AND STRATEGIES

In order to have a clear pricing strategy, it is essential to know your organizational expectations and commitments. The manager of a fee-based information service negotiates its mission and purpose as well as its fiscal responsibilities with the library administration at the outset. Will the service be expected to make a profit? Recover its costs totally or partially? Will the service be required to pay additional overhead to the parent institution? What will happen if there are profits, or conversely, losses? What legal and financial rules apply to the service?

There is no magical formula for setting prices. Your institution and client environment may require a radically different approach to charging than does your colleague in a neighboring library. In order to identify appropriate pricing models, managers of fee for service units need to have a clear understanding of internal and external environments, both within the parent organization and externally within the broader university, city, or state.

What Is the Specific Mission of the Fee-Based Unit?

The mission for many of the original library fee-based services in this country is to support knowledge transfer and economic development. Several of these centers were developed using federal and state grants with the express stipulation to provide direct research assistance to companies and small businesses.

Who Are the Clients to Be Served?

For most academic and public library fee-based information services, their targeted market includes non-primary users of their library—businesses, consultants, law firms. Some services may also choose to offer document delivery and research services to their primary users at discounted fees. Deciding who you serve is a factor in determining what you charge.

Is the Service Expected to Be Cost Recovery? Profit Making? Subsidized?

One of the great myths of fee-based information services is that they are for-profit and they "make money." Truth be told, many fee-based services have healthy beginnings, then close up because they are unable to meet rising costs. It is essential to have a clear concept of the extent of cost recovery that will be assumed. Other questions to consider are what happens to profits, and what happens in a particular year that the service suffers a loss? Will the library administration float you a loan? What exactly are the consequences?

What Are the Organizational Goals of the Fee-Based Unit?

Is the fee-based unit a small, peripheral service, perhaps only filling on-demand document delivery? Or is it a full-service entity providing a broad range of information services from the routine to the unusual? If a service intends to provide in-depth services such as consulting, business analysis, or primary research, the manager needs to be prepared to invest heavily in labor for librarians and other information specialists, and to be able to charge large project-based fees. Bidding too low on a large consulting project can mean many hours of "free" time for the client, and will eat into most of the revenue gained.

PRICING MODELS

Pricing is an art and pricing decisions reflect a blend of intuition, past experience, and sophisticated analysis.[1]

Pricing is never established in a vacuum. Rather it is a dynamic, multi-part process. In addition to reflecting institutional goals, it is also an element of marketing strategy. Setting the right price can lead to a steady income stream. Conversely, pricing too low may generate business, but most likely will not cover expenses. Unforeseen economic fluctuations or unexpected business losses or expensive cash outlays can tilt a service in the red column where it is difficult to turn the service around.

Pricing can serve multiple objectives:

- To recover costs
- To maximize profits and return on capital invested
- To improve or maintain market share
- To keep pace with prices charged by the competition
- To stabilize the going rate
- To control demand

The economic literature is full of pricing theory. Several primary models recur in the literature:

Cost Based Pricing: Based on analyzing total costs to produce products, then pricing to recover costs and add profit margins.

Demand Based Pricing: Operates on the principle that the higher the demand for a product, the higher the price will be.

Competition Based Pricing: Based on following the industry's "going rate" for a product or service.

Optimum or Pricing According to Value: Incorporates several factors to identify a price, including value of the product, needs of the consumer, and market segmentation.

COST ACCOUNTING METHODOLOGY

When I was hired as the director of the University of Colorado Technical Research Center (CTRC) in 1989, I inherited a pricing fiasco. CTRC, in existence since 1967, was working its way into a $20,000 deficit. Prices were very low and staff spent too much time for too little return on their document delivery and research projects. I was given three years to turn the service from red to black or the library administration would seriously consider closing it.

One of the first things I did was to ask the university's accounting office to conduct a unit cost accounting study for CTRC. I needed a way to identify exactly how much it cost to provide each of the services that we offered. The accountant and I developed a methodology based on standard accounting practices and cost accounting principles developed by the federal Office of Management and Budget (OMB) to calculate the indirect cost rate for research.[2] In order to give the accountant the figures she needed to do the calculations, I had to get a clear picture of staff job duties and how much time they spent on different tasks related to our "products" and services. After identifying these service lines, each staff member allocated the time spent on average for each service during a week's time. The spreadsheets looked like the sample in Figure 1.

In addition to staff costs, cost accounting methodology allocates expenses as either direct or indirect costs. Direct costs are those tangible expenses that support day to day operations, including:

- Salaries and benefits
- Photocopy expenses
- ILL payments
- Database fees
- Capital equipment
- Telecommunications
- Mail and postage

FIGURE 1

Employee Name	Total Sal/ben	Doc Del CU	Doc Del ILL	Online Research	Other Research	Copy right	Special Project	Admin Office Support
Doe	15,000	10%		90%				
Smith	24,000	26%	26%		15%	1%	2%	30%
Jones	18,000	40%	10%		5%	5%	25%	15%
Brown	20,500	10%	60%		19%	1%		10%

Indirect costs, listed below, are less tangible. They are often part of the overhead that is charged by some institutions to support their fee-based services.

- Building use, e.g., space, heat, lights
- Equipment use
- Maintenance
- General libraries operational support, e.g., shelving, technology support
- Institutional administrative support, e.g., accounting, personnel

Fee-based information services that follow generally accepted accounting practices and institutional audit rules usually have accounting software to track receivables and payables. This makes it a simple matter of tracking payables into the service lines that will be used as the basis for establishing unit costs. The sample sheet below (Figure 2) without figures provides an outline of this activity.

CTRC's cost accounting study includes many more worksheets than detail the allocation of expenses and revenue to each cost center that is outlined in the examples shown. Contact the author for additional information.[3] Using accounts receivables for the year, you can use the same basic approach for calculating average revenue per job. The difference between average total cost per job and average revenue per job is then expressed as average income (or loss) per job.

In order to undertake a cost accounting study, you must be willing to spend time sorting through all the activities that occur in a fee-based

FIGURE 2

Direct Costs	Total Expenses	Doc Del CU	Doc Del ILL	Online Research	Other Research	Copy-right	Special Project	Admin Office
Support Office supplies	$$$	$$$	$$$	$$$	$$$	$$$	$$$	$$$
Mailing								
Photo-duplications								
ILL payments								
Data proces.								
Connect fees								
Capital equip.								
Admin charges (overhead by Univ.)								

service; tracking down all the expenses incurred; and detailing your business receivables. It is a step-by-step process. Having participated in three cost studies for CTRC and two cost studies for the Association of Research Libraries (ARL) Interlibrary Loan Cost Study, I can honestly say that it can be a complex and vexing undertaking. From my experience I have identified the following steps:

1. Identify each product and service to be analyzed as a cost center.
2. Identify all operating costs as direct or indirect costs.
3. Determine salaries and benefits for each staff member and students.
4. Determine the percentage of time each employee spends on the products and services listed in number 1.
5. Determine the percentage of time each person spends on administrative office support.
6. Assign direct costs to the respective cost centers.
7. Assign other unallocated costs to each cost center.
8. Add total direct costs for each cost center.
9. Allocate indirect costs such as general and administrative expenses to each cost center based on the percentage of each category to 100% (optional).

10. Other overhead costs such as building use, equipment depreciation, etc., can be allocated to each cost center using the same percentage formula above.
11. Total direct and indirect costs minus exclusions or subsidies = grand total costs.
12. To determine the average cost per job, divide the total number of jobs into the grand total costs for each product/service/cost center.

SETTING FEES

We learned a great deal from our first cost accounting study. For example, the data supported what I suspected all along, that staff salaries and benefits were the largest percentage of our costs. We discovered that too much staff time was expended on products that produced very little revenue or, in fact, lost revenue. For example, providing interlibrary loan materials to clients turned out to very labor intensive, so our costs were high, about $34 per ILL document, but our charges were too low and we saw a loss in that product category. On the other hand, our on-campus document delivery, which was easier, less staff intensive and less costly, generated profits. Rather than raise prices significantly in one or two areas, we weighed a number of factors in addition to the cost study in order to raise prices.

MARKET COMPARISONS AND SURVEYS

Once we completed our cost analysis, we did a market comparison of what our colleagues were charging for the same services, and what their fee schedules looked like. We found some with very high prices, and others that were lower than our original fees. We wanted to be priced in the middle range of what the market would bear. We were concerned that charging too high could result in loss of clients who were used to our old prices, while charging too low would keep us in a deficit.

We also conducted a client survey about the same time that we were evaluating our fee structure. The survey told us who our clients were, gave us basic company information–size, number of employees, annual revenues if available, and how they used our services. From these results we determined that most of our clients fell in the engineering, technology, environmental, and biomedical categories. Their information needs included the "harder-to-find" type of document request, e.g., conference proceedings, scientific papers, technical reports.

We facilitated focus group feedback on pricing issues, which told us that pricing fees with lots of add-ons for small amounts, such as postage, verification, and handling, were annoying and disliked. Clients preferred to have base fees that included the cost of providing the item as well as delivering it. We then streamlined our pricing schedule and eliminated many add-ons. Some additional fees will always be necessary, such as rush fees and copyright royalties.

PRICING ACCORDING TO VALUE

In addition to raising prices we took the opportunity to re-evaluate our pricing philosophy. As a labor intensive, value added endeavor, the staff felt strongly that prices should accurately reflect the time and expertise spent locating elusive and incomplete information requests. We discussed how much time could be given away without charging and under what circumstances. We discussed pricing for special, large volume projects at rates discounted from our standard fees. We decided on the time frame that constituted a rush fee. We worked out a simplified pricing schedule so that even student assistants could apply prices as they prepared each day's invoices. We agreed to be flexible so that as circumstances dictated, we could reduce a fee or waive it, for instance if a request was not filled in the client's specified time frame. We left ourselves open to the possibility of price changes if revenue did not cover expenses, or if volume declined. As a manager I also reiterated our service philosophy and mission so that we connected prices to our organizational purpose. We also agreed that our goal for the first years of my tenure was to develop a steady client base with a constant cost recovery income stream.

WHAT IS THE RIGHT PRICE?

Cost studies are an integral part of determining the right price to charge. It may sound too simplistic, but the right price is one that is:

- Not too high or too low
- Reflects the quality of the product and its value
- Recovers the cost of producing the product or service
- Reflects time expended in production
- Is easy to apply and change
- Is flexible and can be changed to match particular situational or client needs

Using all the data we gathered from our cost study and market comparisons we developed several pricing models. Then, using previous years' annual statistics I forecasted projected volume for the coming year and calculated how much revenue we needed in our various service lines in order to break even or make a "profit" that could be re-invested into CTRC. Based on our final price increases, CTRC dramatically turned from being in the red to being in the black within the year. Subsequently each time we undergo a cost study, we tweak our prices, sometime minimally, sometimes only in one product and not in others.

There are many lessons to be learned from cost studies. They can help you identify redundancy, inefficiencies, and staff concerns. The value of a cost study is that it is very black and white and the figures generally do not lie. We have found them to be very reflective of our costs.

In the final analysis, there are three major components to determining the right price. You need to know your goals and objectives, both financial and institutional goals. You need to also know your market and utilize client surveys and market comparisons. Last but not least, you need to know your costs and be able to project expenses and revenue. Then with solid figures, managerial foresight, and strong income streams, most services will withstand economic cycles and continue to offer value to clients and libraries.

NOTES

1. Harriet W. Zais, "Economic Modeling: An Aid to the Pricing of Information Services," *Journal of the American Society for Information Science*, Vol. 28(2): 89-90.

2. "Cost Principles for Educational Institutions," Office of Management and Budget, *OMB Circular No. A-21*.

3. Yem S. Fong, (email *Judith.Fong@colorado.edu*). Sample cost accounting sheets.

REFERENCES

George, Lee Anne. 1996. "The Price is Right: Analyzing Costs in a Fee-Based Information Service." *Fee for Service* 3(2): 7-10.

Herman, Larry. 1990. "Costing, Charging, and Pricing: Related but Different Decisions." *The Bottom Line* 4(2): 26-28.

Olaisen, Johan L. 1989. "Pricing Strategies for Library and Information Services." *Libri* 39(4): 253-274.

Kibirige, Harry M. 1983. *The Information Dilemma: A Critical Analysis of Information Pricing and the Fees Controversy.* Westport, CT: Greenwood Press.

Ward, Suzanne M. 1997. *Starting and Managing Fee-Based Information Services in Academic Libraries.* Greenwich, CT,: JAI Press.

Zais, Harriet W. 1977. "Economic Modeling: An Aid to the Pricing of Information Services." *Journal of the American Society for Information Science* 28(2): 89-95.

Copyright Considerations for Fee-Based Document Delivery Services

Laura N. Gasaway

SUMMARY. Copyright issues command special attention from fee-based service managers. This article provides an overview of copyright law, including the latest information on the 1998 Digital Millennium Copyright Act, and explains how the law affects reproduction of copyrighted works by library fee-based services. It discusses the differences and similarities between interlibrary loan and library document delivery services, and examines issues and situations related to the decision to pay royalties or not. *[Article copies available for a fee from The Haworth Document Delivery Service: 1-800-342-9678. E-mail address: getinfo@haworthpressinc.com <Website: http://www.haworthpressinc.com>]*

KEYWORDS. Fee-based information services, document delivery, copyright, interlibrary loan, legal issues, fair use, non-profit, Digital Millennium Copyright Act, Association of American Publishers, electronic documents

INTRODUCTION

Document delivery has significant copyright implications for libraries. Despite our bias as librarians toward free universal library

Laura N. Gasaway is Director of the Law Library and Professor of Law, University of North Carolina, CB # 3385, Chapel Hill, NC 27599 (Email: laura_gasaway@unc.edu).

[Haworth co-indexing entry note]: "Copyright Considerations for Fee-Based Document Delivery Services." Gasaway, Laura N. Co-published simultaneously in *Journal of Interlibrary Loan, Document Delivery & Information Supply* (The Haworth Information Press, an imprint of The Haworth Press, Inc.) Vol. 10, No. 1, 1999, pp. 75-92; and: *Information Delivery in the 21st Century: Proceedings of the Fourth International Conference on Fee-Based Information Services in Libraries* (ed: Suzanne M. Ward, Yem S. Fong, and Tammy Nickelson Dearie) The Haworth Press, Inc., 1999, pp. 75-92. Single or multiple copies of this article are available for a fee from The Haworth Document Delivery Service [1-800-342-9678, 9:00 a.m. - 5:00 p.m. (EST). E-mail address: getinfo@haworthpressinc.com].

service for all, the reproduction of copyrighted works for outside users raises serious concerns for both content providers and for libraries that strive to follow the law. These copyright issues can be addressed by the organization so that users of the document delivery service are still well served while the document delivery service (DDS) complies with the law.

The following discussion makes several important assumptions.

1. The material reproduced is copyrighted.
2. The DDS provides either single or multiple copies upon request.
3. Users of the service are primarily outside the organization and are "customers."
4. Fees are charged for providing the copy of the document.
5. Fees may be cost recovery or may be greater than just cost recovery.
6. In many instances content providers have valid claims for royalties for reproduction and distribution of their works.

Even with the importance of these issues to both libraries and to copyright holders, to date there has been no litigation involving DDS in non-profit libraries. In fact, there has been only one case involving a commercial DDS.[1] There certainly has been some posturing on the part of the Association of American Publishers (AAP) as evidenced in a position paper it published in 1992.[2] This paper made a number of claims that demonstrated a lack of understanding of the differences in document delivery and interlibrary loan as well as the differences between profit-generating and cost-recovery activities. Further, at best, it overstated the law, and at worst, misstated the copyright law to prove its position that libraries that operated a fee-based DDS were violating the copyright law.[3]

A review of the relevant law, examination of the Association of American Publishers Position Papers, and considerations from the new Digital Millennium Copyright Act[4] provide a foundation for principles that should guide DDS's.

COPYRIGHT LAW BASICS

Copyright law in the United States is grounded in the Constitution which states that "The Congress shall have the Power . . . To promote the Progress of Science and useful arts, by securing for limited times to Authors and Inventors the exclusive Right to their respective Writings and Discoveries."[5] Promoting learning is thus the goal of copyright; it is not a welfare provision for content providers. The rights given to them under the copyright law are all aimed at furthering the public good of promoting learning among the populace. Thus, there is a balancing of rights between copyright owners and users in the law.

Section 102 of the Copyright Act of 1976[6] provides that copyright exists in any original work of authorship that is fixed in tangible media of expression currently known or later developed. Thus, a work is protected by copyright from the time it is created (the mental part of authorship) and transferred to any tangible form such as paper and ink, print, videotape, or computer disk (the physical part). The copyright subsists for life of the author plus 70 years;[7] if there is no personal author, then the term of copyright is 95 years after the date of first publication or 120 years after creation, whichever comes first.[8]

When the copyright holder produces a work, she receives five exclusive rights which may be described as a bundle of five rights: reproduction, distribution, adaptation, performance, and display.[9] The owner may retain all five rights or may transfer some of them or only certain of the rights. For printed works, at a minimum, the copyright holder generally must transfer the reproduction and distribution rights in order for the publisher to publish the work. If the Copyright Act stopped after § 106, users would still have the right to read works without infringing the exclusive rights of the copyright holder, and libraries could still purchase materials or receive them through a gift and lend them to users. The first sale doctrine says that an owner of a copy of a copyrighted work may dispose of that copy however he sees fit, including lending the copy to others.[10] Thus, when libraries lend books and other materials to users they are exercising their rights under the first sale doctrine. The first sale doctrine, however, does not permit libraries to reproduce materials, even for users. There are two important exemptions in the statute that apply to libraries and ensure that reproduction of even copyrighted works for the library itself and for users is permitted under certain conditions.

The first of these conditions is fair use. Fair use is called the safety valve of U.S. copyright law; it is a privilege for someone other than the copyright owner to use a copyrighted work without seeking permission of the copyright owner or paying royalties. In other words, activity that ordinarily would be infringement is excused if the use is fair. Fair use often applies to research and scholarly uses as opposed to commercial uses. Fair use must be judged on a case-by-case basis, so it is difficult to predict whether a particular use is fair or not. Fair use was incorporated into the statute when it was revised in 1976; it states:

> . . . [T]he fair use of a copyrighted work, including such use by reproduction in copies or phonorecords or any other means specified by that section for purposes such as criticism, comment, news reporting, teaching (including multiple copying for classroom use), scholarship or research, is not an infringement of copyright.[11]

The statute then lists four factors that a court must consider when making a determination about whether a particular use is a fair use:

1. Purpose and character of the use,
2. Nature of the copyrighted work,
3. Amount and substantiality used, and
4. Effect on the potential market for or value of the work.[12]

In evaluating *the purpose and character of the use*, courts favor non-profit educational uses over commercial ones. On the other hand, not all uses, even for education, are fair use. In *Marcus v. Rowley*,[13] the court held that when one teacher copied sections of another teacher's cake decorating booklet and incorporated the sections into a short work she developed for her students at a community college, even though the use was for non-profit educational purposes, it was not a fair use.[14] Nor are all commercial uses per se unfair. In *Campbell v. Acuff-Rose*,[15] the U.S. Supreme Court found that even commercial use may be fair under certain circumstances.[16] Courts also continue to favor productive uses, as opposed to those that merely reproduce a copyrighted work. Thus, extensive quoting from a work to produce a criticism of that work is favored over "slavish copying," a term used by courts when they are critical of especially photocopying.

Nature of the copyrighted work focuses on the work itself. The legislative history states that there is a definite difference in reproducing a short news note and in reproducing a full musical score, just because of the nature of the work. Moreover, there are some works that by their nature have no fair use rights attached, such as standardized tests and workbooklets that by their nature are meant to be consumed.[17] Certain types of works have greater fair use rights attached, for example, factual works such as scientific articles.[18]

Amount and substantiality used considers how much of the copyrighted work was used in comparison to the copyrighted work as a whole. Generally, the smaller the amount used, the more likely a court will find the use to be a fair use. There is no bright line, however, for determining if a certain percentage of a work, number of words, or bars of music used qualify as a fair use. It is clear, however, that the larger the portion used of a work, the less likely it is to be fair use. Amount and substantiality also is a qualitative test; even though one takes only a small portion of a work, it still may be too much if what is taken is the "heart of the work."[19]

The fourth fair use factor, *effect on the market for or value of the work,* is the economic test for the copyright holder. Courts use this factor to determine whether there has been economic loss to the owner. Even if the loss an owner incurs from a particular use is not substantial, courts have found that should the loss become great if the practice become widespread, then market effect favors the copyright holder.[20]

Although fair use is available to all types of users including libraries and applies to all of the rights of the copyright holder, librarians do not often have to rely on fair use. The second exemption, called the library exemption, is found in § 108, applies to most of the reproduction and distribution that libraries do.

THE LIBRARY EXEMPTION

All of Section 108 is written so that the library does not have to pay royalties. If the library can operate within the confines of the exemption, then there is no reason to seek permission from copyright owners or pay royalties. Should the library need to go beyond the exemptions in § 108 and § 107 fair use, then it must seek permission and pay royalties if requested. In order to qualify for the § 108 exemption, libraries must meet several criteria.

- First, the section applies to making single copies of works such as a single copy for a user.
- Second, the reproduction and distribution must be made without direct or indirect commercial advantage.

- Third, the library must either be open to the public or to researchers doing research in the same or a similar field.
- Fourth, copies reproduced by the library must contain a notice of copyright.[21]

Each of these criteria has specific implications for document delivery services.

Single as opposed to multiple-copying does not present many problems for the typical DDS. The only wrinkle may be in providing fax copies to users. Too many libraries have both faxed a copy of a requested article to the patron and then mailed the photocopy to the user. Even with a legend on the mailed copy that the recipient agrees to destroy the faxed copy upon receipt of the photocopy, this violates the preamble statement in § 108, a library may provide only single copies to a user. Instead, the library should, on the cover sheet accompanying the fax, include a warning that the recipient should check the transmission received and report any problems within a number of hours, such as 48 or 72. If a problem is reported, the library can re-send the bad pages.

The "direct or indirect commercial advantage"[22] limitation is more problematic. The meaning of this phrase has never been litigated, and the legislative history is not abundantly clear. Certainly, if the library is selling copies of articles and other materials for a profit, there is a commercial advantage. If the library charges a fee for providing copies, but that fee is based solely on cost recovery, to include supplies, personnel costs, mailing or delivery costs, electricity, and the like, the transaction is revenue neutral for the library and there is neither direct nor indirect commercial advantage. Therefore, no royalties are due based on § 108(a).

Even a non-profit library could decide to operate a for-profit DDS to serve business and industry in its area. For this activity, the library must pay royalties. In fact, it could decide to charge a fairly healthy administrative charge in addition to the royalties to compensate the library for its handling of the fee payment. Even if commercial document delivery services could meet the other § 108(a) requirements, they cannot qualify for the § 108 exemption since the entire purpose of providing the copy is commercial advantage to the DDS.

Also, the library's collection must be open to the public or to non-affiliated researchers doing research in a specialized field,[23] and certainly many libraries in non-profit educational institutions as well as public libraries meet this criteria. For other libraries, this criteria might be met even if the collection is not open to the public generally, but by appointment only for qualified users, such as researchers. Libraries that are not open to any outside users have a more difficult time qualifying under this criteria. It could be argued that a library that is not open to outsiders but that will lend any of its published materials through interlibrary loan also qualifies for this exemption, but the matter has never been litigated.

Each copy reproduced must contain a notice of copyright. This newly amended section now states that the reproduction and distribution must contain a notice of copyright that appears on the copy. If there is no notice, then the library may include a legend "Notice: This work may be protected by copyright."[24] In other words, the library no longer has any choice about whether it will use the American Library Association notice stamp or the real copyright notice.

Section 108 provides three subsections dealing with the reproduction and distribution of copies to library patrons. Section 108(d) states that the section's rights of reproduction and distribution apply when the user requests no more than one article from a periodical issue, or one chapter from a book or other collective work.[25] So, when a patron asks the library to provide a copy of an article, etc., the library may supply the request if three conditions are met:

1. The copy must become the property of the user,
2. The library must have no notice that the copy will be used for other than fair use purposes, and
3. The library places the Register's warning on order forms for copies and displays prominently the same warning where orders are placed.[26]

With DDS patrons, the entire assumption is that the copy will become the property of the user. Because the patron more likely is a distant user, there is little opportunity for the user to report any intended use of the material to a staff member even were the library interested. Instead, the statute simply requires that the library have no notice that the user is requesting the copy for non-fair use purposes. The single article from a journal issue restriction could be a problem when the user or client requests more than one article from an issue. DDS's not paying royalties should restrict themselves to one article per periodical issue, one chapter from a book, except as provided by the narrow § 108(e) exemption.

Copies made under § 108(d) must become the property of the user and the library must have no notice that the copy will be used for other than fair use purposes. Additionally, the library must place on the order form and on a sign located where the orders are placed, the Register's warning.[27]

> The copyright law of the United States (Title 17, United States Code) governs the making of photocopies or other reproductions of copyrighted material.
>
> Under certain conditions specified in the law, libraries and archives are authorized to furnish a photocopy or other reproductions. One of these specific conditions is that the photocopy or reproduction is not to be "used for any purpose other than private study, scholarship, or research." If a user makes a request for, or later uses, a photocopy or reproduction for purposes in excess of "fair use," that user may be liable for copyright infringement.
>
> This institution reserves the right to refuse to accept a copying order if, in its judgement, fulfillment of the order would involve violation of copyright law.[28]

Today, libraries need to consider modern ways to provide this warning in advance of providing copies to users. For example, if the library receives the request via email, then a sign at a physical location in the library is not sufficient, and instead, the library should forward an email warning before providing the copy of the article to a user.

Section 108(g)(1) is the second subsection that relates to the reproduction for users done under § 108(d). It places other requirements on the library that is making the copy. For example, the reproduction and distribution rights under this section extend to "isolated and unrelated reproduction and distribution of a single copy."[29] Provision of copies through a DDS to satisfy individual requests are unlikely to be other than "isolated and unrelated." If however, a user should initially request copies of all or several articles from a periodical issue, the DDS should return the request to the user with an indication that the library can provide a copy of only one article from that issue, and that the user should designate which one she wants. The other alternative is for the DDS to pay royalties on the copies beyond the first copy of the first article from that journal issue that the user requests or to require the user to do so.

The exemption found in § 108(d) also applies to copies of the same material on separate occasions.[30] Therefore, the library is not required to retain internal records to determine which items have been requested by someone else. The fact that over time, multiple users request a copy of the item is no problem. In other words, each user is treated as an individual.

On the other hand, the rights of reproduction and distribution granted under § 108(d) also do not apply if the library or its employees is "aware or has substantial reason to believe that it is engaging in related or concerted reproduction of single or multiple copies of materials described in Subsection (d)."[31] Related or concerted reproduction has never been defined by a court. An example might be when a user requests multiple articles from a journal issue and the library refuses to copy more than one article due to the restriction of one article per issue for copying under § 108(d). So, the user comes back each day and requests another article until she has received the entire issue. If the library is aware that it is doing such copying in contravention of the statute, it should refuse to make the copies. If the DDS is paying royalties, then making copies of articles, even all of the article from an issue for a user is not infringement.

Section 108(g)(1) does not exempt the library if it engages in systematic reproduction of single or multiple copies of portions of works described in § 108(d).[32] Systematic copying has not been defined by a court, but there are cases that held that systematic cover-to-cover copying of commercially-produced newsletters in multiple copies was not fair use. There have been some discussions that DDS's are engaged in systematic copying but not as the legislative history describes it. Interlibrary loan networks and other arrangements involving the exchange of photocopies are specifically not systematic.[33]

The most common example of systematic copying is cover-to-cover copying of commercially produced newsletters. Two for-profit entities have been sued for such activity. Although the earlier case settled, *Pasha Publications, Inc. v. Enmark Gas Corp.*,[34] was decided in the Northern District of Texas. The library subscribed to both the printed and fax editions of *Gas Daily*; when each version was received by the company it reproduced copies and distributed to employees. The court held that such activity was not fair and that the company infringed the publisher's copyright.[35] *Television Digest, Inc. v. U.S. Telephone Association*,[36] was a similar case except that the plaintiff, U.S. Telephone Association, is a non-profit trade association that copied the newsletter *Communications Daily* for distribution to its members. The court said that the fact that the plaintiff was non-profit was immaterial. Newsletter copying is not fair use whether the copying entity was for-profit or non-profit.[37]

Section 108(e) provides another exemption for libraries to reproduce an entire work or a substantial portion thereof if certain conditions are met. First, the library must conduct a reasonable investigation to determine that a copy cannot be obtained at a fair price.[38] The legislative history indicates that normally this would require consulting commonly known U.S. trade sources such as wholesalers, retailers, jobbers, etc., contacting the publisher or author, if known, or using an authorized reproducing service, i.e., one that has permission from the copyright owner to reproduce the entire work.[39] Unlike § 108(c), this section even requires searching for a copy of the work from used book stores. After such an investigation turns up no copy of a work at a fair price, then the library may reproduce a copy of it for a user. Then the three requirements from § 108(d) also must be met: (1) the copy must become the property of the user, (2) the library must have no notice that the copy will be used for other than scholarship, research, teaching, etc., and (3) the library provides the user with the Register's warning in advance of providing the copy.[40]

IS INTERLIBRARY LOAN DOCUMENT DELIVERY?

In the broadest sense interlibrary loan (ILL) is a type of document delivery. Traditionally, however, ILL is a library-to-library transaction, but the newer ILL systems that provide copies directly to end-users blur this distinction somewhat. Publishers have suggested that if the library charges for an ILL transaction, the fees create a commercial advantage for the library. Most libraries that charge for ILL transactions simply use the fees to cover a small portion of the copying, mailing, and staff costs. Very few libraries conduct ILL operations even to provide cost recovery, much less to make a profit.

ILL is permitted under the § 108(g)(2) proviso that states:

. . . Nothing in this clause prevents a library or archives from participating in interlibrary arrangements that do not have as their purpose of effect receipt of copies in such aggregate quantities as to substitute for a subscription to or purchase of a work.

The CONTU interlibrary loan guidelines[41] then go on to specify what are such aggregate quantities to substitute for a subscription to or purchase of a work. The guidelines say that each year a borrowing library may make five requests from a periodical title going back over the most recent five years (60 months). The guidelines take no position on materials older than five years. If the library either owns the title but it is missing from its collection, or if the title is on order, the library does not count the ILL copy in its suggestion of five. If the work is not a periodical, the library may make five requests per year for the entire life of the copyright. The borrowing library must maintain records for three calendar years. The lending library's responsibility is to require a certification that the request conforms to the guidelines.[42]

As libraries have been forced to cancel expensive journal titles because of escalating costs, many are relying on both ILL and document delivery to provide access to materials for their users. In fact, academic libraries now often are members of the Copyright Clearance Center (CCC) and directly pay royalties for ILL copies beyond the suggestion of five or from a document delivery service that is not paying the royalties. Libraries may determine that the better alternative is to order the copies for articles beyond the five permitted in the guidelines from a DDS that handles the royalties. The decision as to the route to pursue is based most often on the need for speed, the charges of the document delivery service, and the like. Because libraries are now using both commercial and noncommercial DDS as well as ILL, often these concepts are blurred since the end result for the requesting library is the same: The user receives copies of requested materials, and royalties are paid for copies in excess of the ILL guidelines.

Libraries themselves may have caused some of the blurring of the distinction between traditional interlibrary loan and document delivery. Often these two operations are performed in the same section of the library and it may be called the DDS. Libraries may be better advised to keep the distinction between ILL and document delivery differentiated for the library so that staff and clients understand the difference.

A further complicating factor is whether the library pays DDS royalties for its commercial clients while not doing so for ILL requests that it fills from its collection. The borrowing library is responsible for staying within the CONTU guidelines and therefore for paying royalties for copies obtained beyond the suggestion of five. So, when a lending library treats the two activities differently for purposes of copyright royalties, there is no problem with liability. There may, however, be a management difficulty in training staff to recognize the difference and to fulfill the requirements of the statute.

ELECTRONIC COPIES

May a DDS provide electronic copies of printed works to its clients as opposed to photocopies? The Copyright Act itself is technology neutral. It always uses the word "reproduce" as opposed to "photocopy," and many argue that providing an electronic copy to a user is permitted under the library exemption as long as the other requirements of §§ 108(d)-(e) are met. Because one of these requirements is that the copy become the property of the user, the library would not be permitted to maintain a database of scanned articles to use for providing electronic copies in lieu of scanning an article in response to a particular request from a user.

Another consideration, however, is the fact that the CCC has not generally been licensed by publishers to collect royalties for electronic copies. Thus, if the DDS wanted to pay copyright royalties for their clients, individual permission would have to be obtained from publishers. Further, the AAP has stated its express disapproval of scanning as a method to provide copies of documents.[43]

Assuming that these concerns could be solved, there is a question about electronic delivery of copies. The DDS could email the electronic copy to the client or it might consider posting the article on a password-protected Website. The Web posting is likely to raise more concerns on the part of publishers, but the DDS could develop a procedure to post the article, deliver the password to the client, and then remove the article from the Web as soon as the client has downloaded the article. The problem with this activity is that, in effect, it involves multiple rather than single copying. One could argue, of course, that the end result is the same: The client ends up with one copy and the other copies are simply incidental to making that copy, and the incidental copies disappear.

Publishers are also likely to be concerned that converting their materials to HTML format compromises the integrity of the information. Therefore using PDF format which discourages alteration of the data may be preferable.

Before deciding to undertake such a project, however, the DDS should be aware of *CARL v. Ryan*.[44] CARL UnCover operates a commercial document delivery service. It charges its clients both for the service of providing copies and for royalties that it pays to the copyright holder. Even if the end user's use is fair use, CARL still charges for and pays royalties. Over the years CARL has negotiated agreements with publishers to permit it to scan articles whenever a client requests a particular article so it can provide either a faxed or printed copy to the client. When another client requests the same article, CARL then uses its database to provide the copy, but it still pays royalties for the reproduction. All of this is done under agreements with publishers.[45]

CARL was sued by freelance authors because they were not receiving royalties for reproductions of their articles. Instead, publishers received the royalties from CARL. Authors argued that either they transferred to publishers the right to sell individual copies of articles or their individual permission was required for CARL to be able to sell individual copies of articles.[46] CARL relied on *Tasini v. New York Times Co.*[47] that also concerned the relationship between freelance writers and their publishers. In this case, writers argued that they were entitled to additional royalties when publishers now made their journals available in electronic format in addition to print. When writers transferred reproduction and distribution rights, electronic journals were not envisioned, and the transfers were silent about electronic rights.[48]

The *Tasini* court held that publishers could include freelance authors' entire collected works in databases without permission or further compensation to authors. The court held that conversion to electronic format was a permissible revision to the collected work.[49]

In *CARL*, the court found that *Tasini* was inapplicable. It agreed that authors retained all rights not specifically transferred. While publishers owned the rights in the collective work, such as the journal issue, all they could grant to CARL was the right to reproduce the entire collective work and not individual author contributions.[50] This was contrasted with *Tasini* where the publishers were creating electronic versions of the journal and not copying individual articles.[51] Carl UnCover has indicated that the suit will be appealed. If CARL is upheld, then a library operating a for-profit DDS will have to deal with individual authors as well as publishers. In the long run, publisher agreements with authors will probably cover making individual copies of articles available, but such agreements are not likely to be retrospective. Despite creation of the Authors Registry[52] for handling permissions and royalties for individual authors, this situation will likely discourage many DDS's.

Another important question arises when the DDS is asked to provide a copy of an article from an electronic journal to which the library subscribes. In that instance the license agreement will control, and the library is bound by the terms of that agreement. When negotiating licenses, libraries should clarify whether e-journals to which they subscribe may be used for traditional ILL and for document delivery to paying clients. It might be possible to negotiate a two-tiered agreement, for example, one that provided one rate and a set of conditions for non-profit educational use by students, faculty, and staff at a university and a different rate for document delivery to outside entities.

TO PAY OR NOT TO PAY ROYALTIES

Libraries that provide document delivery services may or may not have to pay royalties to copyright holders to compensate for these reproductions of copyrighted works. There are three possible alternatives:

> 1. The DDS operates on a cost-recovery basis and expects the client to compensate copyright holders if royalties are due;
> 2. The DDS operates on a cost-recovery basis but determines that, as a part of its service to outside clients, it will include royalty fees in its charges and then pay royalties to the Copyright Clearance Center or directly to the copyright holder, or
> 3. The DDS operates as a for-profit center within the non-profit library and must pay royalties.

As previously discussed, one important factor is whether the library makes a profit on its document delivery activity or whether the fees it charges are cost recovery or less. Even if the library itself operates its DDS on a cost-recovery basis, the client of the DDS may still have to pay royalties to the copyright holders for reproductions of protected works. For example, if the client is in a for-profit library that has a Copyright Clearance Center license for in-house copying, it must pay individually for copies of works obtained from outside entities. Many libraries in the for-profit sector prefer to do business with a DDS that handles the royalties as a part of its service. However, should the company use a library DDS that charges fees only at the cost-recovery level for the service, then the end-user, the requesting entity, must ensure that permission is sought and royalties paid if due. This raises a question of what the DDS should do to alert clients that they are responsible for any royalties. Some DDS's stamp each article reproduced with a legend to the effect that if royalties are due for the copy, the client is responsible for them. A for-profit DDS that pays royalties for clients is more likely to mark copies of articles with a legend "royalties cleared" or "royalties paid."

A number of DDS's have determined that even if their fees provide cost recovery only, they will offer to take care of the royalties as a part of their services. Not only do they charge their regular fee to the client, but they also include fees for the royalties and even an additional administrative charge for taking care of the copyright royalties and record keeping. These DDS's generally establish accounts with the CCC.

CONCLUSION

In his excellent book chapter on ILL, DDS, and recent litigation, James S. Heller suggests some guidelines for libraries that operate a DDS.[53] With one change necessitated due to the Digital Millennium Copyright Act, the guidelines remain a good advice for today.

- The library pays royalties when appropriate regardless of whether the work is registered with the Copyright Clearance Center.
- The library limits copying to one copy for a user without paying royalties.
- Multiple copying for a user is done only when royalties are paid.
- The library limits copying to no more than half of a periodical issue without seeking permission and paying royalties.

- If the library faxes the copy to a user, the library destroys the incidental photocopy made.
- If the library sends the user a digital copy, the library does not retain a digital copy for itself.
- A library that requests materials through ILL follows the CONTU guidelines.
- Lending libraries do not provide ILL copies if they know that the request exceeds the CONTU guidelines.[54]

Only the final guideline must be changed based to reflect the new requirements on reproducing the copyright notice that appears on the work. Heller recommends that copies be stamped with, "This material may be protected by Copyright Law (Title 17, U.S. Code)." Due to the changes effected by the Digital Millennium Copyright Act, each copy must reproduce the actual copyright notice and use the legend Heller suggests only if there is no notice on the work.[55]

There are benefits to DDS's that simply handle the royalties for all clients as a part of the service they provide. Others find it more advantageous to expect the client to take care of any royalties due to the copyright holder for reproduction of articles. Whether a library DDS determines that including the payment of royalties is a service it wants to offer depends on a number of factors. Some considerations might be:

- Whether clients are willing to pay an administrative charge to reimburse the DDS for its efforts,
- Whether the library has combined a DDS and ILL into the same management unit,
- The scope of the library's collection,
- Level of DDS activity,
- Advertising activity or plans for such, and
- Client demands.

Since a DDS in a non-profit library is only one unit of a complex organization rather than the entire business of a commercial service, the decisions made about how to handle the copyright issues may vary from one library to another.

One thing remains clear. If the DDS operates on a fee schedule that is greater than cost recovery, then the library is receiving a commercial advantage for this activity and it has moved outside of the § 108 library exemption and it must pay royalties.

REFERENCES

1. *Ryan v. Carl Corp.*, 23 F. Supp.2d 1146 (N. D. Cal.1998).

2. Association of American Publishers, *AAP Position Paper on Commercial and Fee-Based Document Delivery* (1992).

3. *Id.*

4. Pub. L. 105-304, signed October 28, 1998.

5. U.S. Const. Art. I, § 8 (1994).

6. 17 U.S.C. §§ 101-1332 (1994, *as amended* by Pub. L. 105-298, October 27, 1998 and Pub. L. 105-304, October 28, 1998).

7. *Id.* § 302(a), *as amended by* Pub. L. 105-298, October 27, 1998.

8. *Id.* § 302(c).

9. *Id.* § 106.

10. *Id.* § 109(a).

11. *Id.* § 107.

12. *Id.* § 107(1)-(4).

13. 695 F.2d 1711 (9th Cir. 1983).

14. *Id.* at 178-79.

15. *Luther Campbell a/k/a Luke Skywalker v. Acuff-Rose Music, Inc.*, 510 U.S. 569 (1994). In this case the rap group Two Live Crew produced a music parody of the Roy Orbison hit "Pretty Woman."

16. Because the rap group sold the CD on which the song parody was found, the use of the copyrighted Orbison song was a commercial use. The Court stated that even a commercial use may be a fair use. *Id.* at 584-85.

17. S. Rept. No. 460, 94th Cong., 1st Sess. (1975), *reprinted in* 13 *Omnibus Copyright Revision Legislative History 64* (1977).

18. *American Geophysical Union v. Texaco, Inc*, 37 F.3d 881, 893 (2d Cir. 1994).

19. *Harper & Row Publishers v. Nation Enterprises.*, 471 U.S. 539, 564-65 (1985).

20. *Texaco*, 37 F.3d 896.

21. 17 U.S.C. § 108(a) (1994).

22. *Id.* § 108(a)(1).

23. *Id.* § 108(a)(2).

24. *Id.* § 108(a)(3), as amended by P.L. 105-304, § 404, Oct. 28, 1998.

25. *Id.* § 108(d).

26. *Id.*

27. *Id.*

28. 37 C.F.R. § 201.14 (1998).

29. *Id.* § 108(g)(1).

30. *Id.*

31. *Id.* § 108(g)(1).

32. *Id.*

33. H. Rept. No. 1476, 94th Cong., 2d Sess. (1975), *reprinted in* 17 *Omnibus Copyright Revision Legislative History 77-78* (1977) [hereinafter House Report].

34. 22 U.S.P.Q.2d 1076 (N.D. Tex. 1992).

35. *Id*. at 1076-77.

36. 47 P.T.C.J. 32 (D.D.C. 1993).

37. *Id*. at 33.

38. 17 U.S.C. § 108(e) (1994).

39. House Report, *supra* note 33, at 76.

40. 17 U.S.C. § 108(e) (1994).

41. Conf. Rept. 94-1733 2d Sess. (1975), *reprinted in* 17 *Omnibus Copyright Revision Legislative History* 71-74 (1977).

42. *Id*. 72-73.

43. *See* Association of American Publishers, *AAP Position Paper on Scanning* (1994).

44. 23 F. Supp.2d 1146 (N. D. Cal.1998).

45. *Id*. at 1147.

46. *Id*. at 1149.

47. 972 F. Supp. 804 (S.D.N.Y. 1997).

48. *Id*. at 806.

49. *Id*. at 826-27.

50. *Carl*, 23 F. Supp.2d, at 1149-50.

51. *Id*. at 1150.

52. See *http://www.webcom/registry*

53. James S. Heller, "The Impact of Recent Litigation on Document Delivery and Interlibrary Loan," in Laura N. Gasaway, *Growing Pains: Adapting Copyright for Libraries, Education and Society* 189, 212-15 (1997).

54. *Id*. at 212-14.

55. 17 U.S.C. § 108(a)(3)(1994), as amended by Pub. L. 105-304, § 404, October 28, 1998.

The Future for Information Professionals: Back to the Future

Amelia Kassel

ABSTRACT. This paper explores the changing role of the information professional in a dynamic environment in which technology, resources, information needs, and user expectations change very rapidly. The author's conclusion is that while some of the roles of traditional librarians may be disappearing, there are plenty of opportunities for proactive information professionals in the new information environment. There are new services, new expertise, and new job titles. Businesspeople recognize that technology is not everything; the human factor, a person to select, filter, and analyze information, is critical. Information brokers and library fee-based service staff stand at the forefront of this new environment, because they are already used to employing and continually improving these vital skills. *[Article copies available for a fee from The Haworth Document Delivery Service: 1-800-342-9678. E-mail address: getinfo@haworthpressinc.com <Website: http://www.haworthpressinc.com>]*

KEYWORDS. Future of librianship. information needs, user expectations, knowledge management, fee-based information services, information brokers, business enviroment, skills, opportunities

INTRODUCTION

This article is based on an address given to the Fourth International Conference on Fee-Based Information Services in Libraries, Novem-

Amelia Kassel is affiliated with MarketingBASE, USA, Information Broker and Expert Online Research, Consulting & Training, Information Broker Mentor Program (Email: amelia@marketingbase.com).

[Haworth co-indexing entry note]: "The Future for Information Professionals: Back to the Future." Kassel, Amelia. Co-published simultaneously in *Journal of Interlibrary Loan, Document Delivery & Information Supply* (The Haworth Information Press, an imprint of The Haworth Press, Inc.) Vol. 10, No. 1, 1999, pp. 93-105; and: *Information Delivery in the 21st Century: Proceedings of the Fourth International Conference on Fee-Based Information Services in Libraries* (ed: Suzanne M. Ward, Yem S. Fong, and, Tammy Nickelson Dearie) The Haworth Press, Inc., 1999, pp. 93-105. Single or multiple copies of this article are available for a fee from The Haworth Document Delivery Service [1-800-342-9678, 9:00 a.m. - 5:00 p.m. (EST). E-mail address: getinfo@haworthpressinc.com].

93

ber 1997. Since that time, the information industry, technology, and the roles of librarians and information professionals have continued to expand. Library and business literature on the subject that elaborates about changing roles has been added. As a result, it was pertinent to research this subject for the latest thinking and to incorporate some parts of my original presentation with current applicable literature as a way to augment and, hopefully, to enrich my initial ideas about "The Future for Information Professionals."

THE NEW WORLD

During the past three chaotic years, Internet service providers, online consumer services, and Web browsers first proliferated and then consolidated. Search engines, originally geared to the consumer mass market for quick and easy use, grew in numbers, complexity, and refinements and became essential research tools for information professionals, although not without shortcomings. This last year has seen Internet-only databases popping up, traditional database producers peeling away from commercial vendors to form their own Web databases, and all major traditional online services joining the bandwagon to roll out browser-based access.[1] New software products, generically called intelligent agents, are now available for tracking, organizing, and filtering information and some information professionals are experimenting with them. Of greatest significance, Web content has exploded, making the Internet a truly rich and necessary tool for finding resources and information never before online. Wise information professionals today know that they must conduct Internet research, although, unlike end-users, they also keep up on the multitude of content offerings and must distinguish between sources that best meet an information need–something which depends not only on content but also on time and cost efficiencies.

THE DEMISE OF INFORMATION PROFESSIONALS?

In past years, some librarians felt doomed. Naysayers amongst the profession, usually librarians themselves, were sure that the whole field would just evaporate. There is probably some good justification for this attitude since we have seen cutbacks and closures of libraries and deep slashes in academic and public library budgets. Library schools have also shut, making many in the field wonder what would become of the profession. Again and again, we have heard that some form of computer technology, such as artificial intelligence or robots, would soon replace human beings, especially in view of the seeming Internet takeover of the world. To some, it looked as though these electronic brains would combine together with the Web–whose users now rank in the hundreds of millions–to replace highly trained and skilled librarians. What librarian has not faced a comment like, "If it's not on the Net, it must not exist," and then has wanted to pull her hair out because of knowledge to the contrary? A relatively common question to information brokers is, "What's happening to your business now that everyone has access to the Internet?" The implication is that information professionals are condemned to oblivion.

Despite all this movement and amid serious concerns, many information professionals are transforming themselves and adapting to the times. Based on personal experience, and that of other successful information brokers, my observation is that we are all busier than ever, although not without the need to expand on the basic skills we learned in library school and to add new capabilities to our repertoire. For some, it also has been necessary to shift previous service offerings and derive new clients–and income–by providing or developing more complex information products or services, since many customers now meet some of their own basic information needs through the resources on the Web. On the other hand, once users experiment with the Internet, many return to the fold, realizing that their expertise lies elsewhere and that their time is better served by choosing to place more detailed and complex research needs into the hands of experts.

One information industry consultant, Susan Feldman, discusses why information professionals need not consider themselves in danger in her article "Our Imminent Demise: Is There A Future for Information Professionals?"[2] She asserts that by analyzing some of the basic skills performed by information professionals a case can be made that counteracts the gloom and doom that some feel. These include:

- Problem Analysis–Librarians are given problems and must identify the central pieces of each problem and the most likely way it can be solved by finding missing information. They know the right questions to ask and how to ask.

- Word Skills–Searching, whether online or offline, requires the ability to explain a subject both in terms of what a human and what a computer can understand. Librarians not only identify synonyms but also know which terms will dilute the search. They understand the structure of words.
- Knowledge of Resources–Librarians collect resources as starting places, not as answers. The ability to know where to find answers, not facts, distinguishes them from amateurs.
- Information Collecting Skills–Librarians know how to use systems and collect the information.
- Interpersonal Skills–Librarians are effective as intermediaries between the client and the information. This requires knowing how to ask questions and to elicit information without being threatening.
- Assessing information for quality, utility, and accuracy.
- Organizing information in patterns and relationships.
- Presenting information so that it is understandable, accessible, and usable.

NEW OPPORTUNITIES– INTERNET RESEARCH

Feldman's skill list indicates important capabilities possessed by information professionals that are not easily or completely replaced by computer technology. In addition, such skills are necessary for deriving solutions. At the same time, it is becoming clearer that new opportunities abound. T. R. Halvorson, attorney and information broker, discusses the "duty to search the Web" in *Internet Opportunities and Liabilities of Information Professionals: Painting the Golden Gate Bridge*.[3] He points to a 1995 lawsuit in the securities industry, "Whirlpool Financial Corp. v. GN Holdings, Inc. 67 F.3d 605 (7th Circ. 1995)." Mary Cornaby, law librarian, explains:

> Responsibility for information available on the Internet also may extend to clients and have a direct impact on their claims. In Whirlpool Financial Corp. v. GN Holdings, Inc., n54 the Seventh Circuit defined the legal consequences of failing to take advantage of information available on the Internet. In that case, the plaintiff claimed that the maker of a defaulted note failed to disclose enough about pending litigation and used fraudulent

projections in the original prospectus. Responding to the defendant's argument that the claims were time-barred under existing case law, the court held that discrepancies between actual and projected results should have placed a reasonable investor on notice that fraud was possible. At the time, the investor should have been aware of the fraud potential because the information it needed to "uncover" the fraud was already publicly available on the Internet. The court stated: In today's society, with the advent of the "information superhighway," federal and state legislation and regulations, as well as information regarding industry trends, are easily accessed. A reasonable investor is presumed to have information available in the public domain, and therefore Whirlpool is imputed with constructive knowledge of this information. The court charged the plaintiff with knowledge of information that was available readily only on the Internet . . . [This case indicates] that information considered easily accessible, or publicly available, now includes electronic sources of information. While a client might not be held to knowledge of what might be available on LEXIS or WESTLAW (although a lawyer certainly could be so charged) . . . the availability of that same information on an Internet site at low or no cost suggests that both clients and their lawyers need to know what is available.[4]

This court decision opens a new avenue for information professionals who can now proactively seek clients based on a legal standard that certain knowledge is a *requirement* for conducting important business transactions.

NEW SERVICES– TRACKING AND MONITORING

Internet tracking or monitoring is on the upswing. In one situation, the corporate communications department of a Fortune 500 company asked an information broker to track five of the company's own brands on the Internet. The company wanted all news stories and Internet discussions about them. There had been controversy regarding their products and news stories were bound to appear in traditional media whereas dialogue amongst the public could possibly be found "somewhere" on the Internet. The CEO wanted information on his desk by 10 a.m. each day during a four month period to help direct official company response. After a reference interview that educated the user about what finding "everything" on the Internet could mean in terms of time and cost–which is how the original question was presented–the information broker helped define and narrow expectations and selected sources. These sources included two specialty search engines for finding electronic discussions on the Internet–Dejanews [www.dejanews.com/corp] and Reference.COM [www.reference.com], three of the largest search engines, and one of the major free Internet-based news services. DejaNews covers 80,000 discussion forums, including Usenet newsgroups; Reference.COM contains more than 150,000 newsgroups, mailing lists, and web forums. Metasearch engines could also have been added to this list had there been more time and budget to handle the project. In addition to Internet research, searches were run in Lexis-Nexis, Dialog, and Dow Jones Interactive for maximum coverage of current news stories. The information broker filtered results for relevancy. On some days only a few pages of information were found and on other days up to 100 pages of articles and pertinent discussions were located and faxed.

In the past, corporate librarians typically counted current alerting as a major library service. Undoubtedly, it is in greater demand now that the Internet is used as a communications and research tool. Companies must pay attention to what former employees, customers, and competitors are saying about them and they also want to know as much about their competitors as possible. Indeed, the field of "competitor intelligence" has grown up during the past fifteen years opening up more opportunities for information professionals.

THE CARBON FACTOR (HUMANS)

Internet tracking and monitoring is quite demanding. It can also involve customizing deliverables for each user or client according to individual desires and needs. Some corporate librarians have established programs or assigned staff to handle demand, whereas some companies outsource such projects to information brokers as in the previous example. Importantly, Rosanne Macek and Karen Draper refer to the advantages of "carbon-based" or what Draper explains is the "human filter."[5] At their organization, Bay Networks, Draper is Manager of Awareness Services. Her job title, in itself, is significant and reflects responsibility for one type of specialty information service that has grown out of the critical need to keep up-to-date on events that could affect a company's activities and direction. Macek and Draper suggest that this type of work is best served with carbon-based agents–yes–librarians (this author's interjection) who are superior in a number of ways to automated technologies and who:

- Filter generic terms.
- Determine "good" and "bad" news.
- Differentiate between articles that are major and those that are not.
- Distinguish between articles with additional information and those that add nothing new.
- Handle sensitive news that should be treated in a special way.
- Select and abstract "top" news.
- Target specific audiences with particular types or sources of news.

NEW EXPERTISE

Some of these recent jobs are found only within the context of fee-based services in libraries, corporate libraries, or outsourcing to information brokers. Yet some newer roles are also becoming routine in public, academic, and college libraries. Many librarians are currently immersed in a transition and pioneer new ground as the current information industry takes shape. As they fashion their environments, they widen their responsibilities, capabilities, and services to a greater extent than ever before. Anthea Stratigos and David Curle of Outsell Inc. [www.outsellinc.com] describe some of the critical roles being played in this new era:[6]

- Buying and Selling Content–Information professionals have developed the skills necessary to evaluate content for use in their own intermediary role and negotiate with vendors.
- Creating Value Added Research–Now that end-users have desktop tools for answering their own routine reference questions, librarians can apply their research skills to a more valuable product. They are creating content such as technology, competitive, and market assessments that answer the "so what?" questions. They provide not just filtered searches but insight that answers

the question–is there a market, how will our technology compete, what should our competitive positioning be?

- Educating Users–End-users need training to guide them through the content they do have, and to make them aware of other content that can help them solve the business problems and decisions they face. All of those needs have led to a greater educational role for information professionals.
- Making Content Available Using Technology–A recent Outsell Inc. survey of a group of corporate librarians revealed that fifty-five percent of them were part of an Intranet development team. Thirty percent of them had a lead role in Intranet development, while IT departments had the lead role in sixty-five percent of the companies represented.

NEW JOBS AND NEW JOB TITLES

If the gloom and doom bunch is not yet convinced about the bright future and opportunities for those of our vocation, let's take a look at some new job descriptions. A list of twenty hot careers includes Info-Seekers, a category that encompasses two relatively new job titles: Corporate Intelligence Officer and Knowledge Manager.[7] Although Knowledge Manager is more closely akin to and, in particular, requires a degree in library science, it is not beyond reason for those with "librarian" skills also to become corporate intelligence officers–*if* they add training and experience in market research and analysis. The Knowledge Manager salary ranges from $50,000 to $90,000 and the Corporate Intelligence Officer starts at $69,000 and goes to $100,000 for Vice President of Corporate Intelligence. Here are the descriptions for each:

- *Knowledge Manager.* "Imagine the old-time corporate librarian. Now trade in her gray flannel skirt and sensible cardigan for a DKNY outfit and triple-pierced ears. That's the difference between an information specialist and its latest variant, the knowledge manager. The makeover comes courtesy of high-tech methods of communicating. Suddenly, says Carla O'Dell, president of the American Productivity & Quality Center in Houston, people know what they don't know and want to become more informed

. . . Now corporations are trying to capture that information on their databases. The knowledge officer is the one who figures out how and what to collect and where to store it. The job blends a working knowledge of classic ways to dig up information (books and magazines) with the Internet, Intranets, databases, and networks, so that ideally anyone in a company can find out anything relevant to her job."

• *Corporate Intelligence Officer.* "Forget any delusions that this job involves cloak-and-dagger undercover operations. Corporate intelligence staffers comb through perfectly legitimate sources of information–newspapers, competitors' sales material, speeches, credit reports, databases, and interviews–for details of competitors' financial conditions. The idea is to monitor the moves of a company's industry competitors and forecast future trends. The job may also involve examining acquisition targets to make sure their business is healthy. Business intelligence officers must not only gather information but also analyze it and explain what it means to top executives."

Perhaps some will shed a tear when they learn that this same article includes a section called the "not-so-hot-careers" and that–yes–you guessed it–Librarian is on the list. Specifically, it says "Librarian: Smaller city, school, and college budgets will slow hiring." If this is true, these institutions and their support mechanisms have yet to follow suit to keep pace with the rest of the universe. And, despite this continuing problem, it appears that the "librarian" appellation, which has always had an image problem that reflected an unwelcome stereotype, continues in its decline–*but*–the profession as a whole is hot as it shifts and grows.

RECOGNITION AT LAST

In an example that illustrates respect and acknowledgment of a librarian's value, the CEO of one corporation meets with the librarian weekly to discuss information that the librarian has gathered. The CEO wants her insights and says that these meetings lead to important results. In a lengthy article, senior editor for *Inc. Magazine*, Leigh Buchanan, explains: "To pinpoint elusive business trends among eclectic, nonquantitative sources of data, CEO Duncan Highsmith depends on a powerful knowledge-management tool–his librarian." Buchanan tells the story of how "both the CEO and the librarian scan newspapers, magazines, books, Web sites, ads and TV and radio programs. They meet weekly to share their impressions and pinpoint trends. The Payoff: the CEO believes that if people at Highsmith have access to the right information, they can help the company anticipate and take advantage of changes."[8] Outsell Inc.'s Stratigos and Curle provide additional insight about the corporate library's value when they explain that "in some cases, information professionals and entire libraries are moving functionally to report to marketing departments. This is a great move and gets this vital corporate function out of the human resources, facilities and the administrative units that have been dead ends for many information centers." Buchanan supports this point in theory when he describes how Highsmith's organization chart is "prominently displayed outside the lunchroom [with] the library . . . on the same line as marketing, human resources, accounting and finance, business-systems development, and–perhaps most sweetly–information systems."

CONFLICT AND STRESS

Admittedly, change causes anxiety and conflict–especially so much chaotic change for those who find themselves in the midst of the information revolution. Nevertheless, information professionals are smart, flexible, and resilient. Arthur Winzenried explains that

> Information professionals are facing more stress than ever before . . . However, the majority are prepared to work and actively seek new skills, new technologies, and new visions . . . There is a future role of information professionals both in industry and education, and it is an increasingly important one. Too often the personal aspect of information provision is overlooked in the light of the dramatic development of technology. However, behind every technological advance, there is a provider whose role it is to source, organize, and disseminate information gleaned by that technology.[9]

Winzenreid also suggests that the need for the information professional is "still present in the need for an intermediary who accesses, assimilates, reformulates, and packages information in a form to suit the user if meaningful outcomes are to be achieved."

INFORMATION BROKERS AND FEE-BASED SERVICES IN LIBRARIES

Up until now discussion has focused on the positive future for librarians. To depart from this theme for a moment, a short history about information brokers and fee-based information services in libraries depicts particular segments of the profession who have been involved in pioneering efforts for some time. From this writer's perspective, the early endeavors of these industry trailblazers have laid a foundation that is now coming to fruition. As the world goes online, savvy users with a thirst for information and knowledge are discovering the value of those who have the skills to create, manage, and organize information–and retrieve and apply it to specific situations for problem solving and decision making. Briefly, the PC revolution of the early eighties made it possible for those with inside knowledge and skills to conduct online research from home or office. Simultaneously, online databases began to grow in number and type–from bibliographic databases to fulltext databases, from a handful to thousands. Information brokering within this context began as an alternative career for librarians who were willing to take a risk. This new breed of independent information professionals led the way by conducting in-depth, high level research projects. Their clientele included, for example, consultants, small professional businesses such as attorneys, public relations firms, or advertising agencies and Fortune 500 companies who wanted to outsource some of their research. Others in this field became database developers, library consultants, and consultants to the information industry itself. Information brokers, some of whom had been operating even prior to the desktop revolution, are now recognized as leaders and marketers for the industry. At about the same time, fee-based services in libraries began to grow, although some fee-based document delivery services were around as early as the 1940s. Fee-based services were established to meet demand by the community beyond "basic" library service with the hope of also creating added revenue to some of the already-reduced budgets. It is not within the scope of this article to dissect success or failure of these alternative forms of service, but is important to recognize that those involved proceeded to build new business and service models. They continue to do so despite controversy within the profession that existed when they started and that lasts to this day to some extent. Information brokers, for example, were criticized for charging fees when the central approach to library services had been equal access to information and free public libraries based on the Carnegie model. Technology is expensive, however, and an unfortunate fact of life is that publicly supported libraries can not (and should not) offer costly services. By creating a new fee-based model, a previously unserved portion of the population–those who can afford payment for services rendered–were now provided for. Fee-based information services in libraries enhance institutional image and make members of the business community aware of the value of their local library. This factor alone has implications for attracting more support to traditional library services.

CONCLUSION

Information professionals are the most important asset in the information retrieval and delivery process. We create the knowledge structure and use it to provide quality and value. Information professionals have constructed new jobs to take advantage of opportunities and meet demand. We have recognized the Web's huge potential and are harnessing it to create unprecedented services. We are a creation of our own invention. If we value who we are and what we do–and proactively promote our immense worth–those who have migrated away will return along with many others. Out of the recent chaos, a whole new industry has evolved that requires many of the same skills that librarians learned at one time, plus new ones too, and some yet to embark upon. Both old-timers and the younger generation are involved. For those who have been willing to change with the times, a pendulum swing has occurred. Many information professionals have already seen this bright new future and are "back to the future" as a result of developing new attitudes, building new business models, shrewdly applying technology, and launching new relationships. These major transformations, taken all together, make up the exciting future for information professionals.

NOTES

1. Kassel, Amelia. "Dialog Alternatives: A Power Searcher's Checklist." *SEARCHER, The Magazine for Database Professionals*, September, 1998, pp. 31-56 [http://www.infotoday.com/searcher/sep/kassel.htm].

2. Feldman, Susan. "Our Imminent Demise. Is There a Future for Information Professionals," *Information Broker*, Nov/Dec 1996. [http://www.burwellinc.com/samplenewsletter2.html].

3. Halvorson, T. R. *Internet Opportunities and Liabilities of Information Professionals: Painting the Golden Gate Bridge.* Burwell Enterprises, 1999. Based on a paper delivered at the 12th Annual Conference of the Association of Independent Information Professionals, 1998. [http://www.netins.net/showcase/trhalvorson/pubs/index.html or http://burwellinc.com].

4. Cornaby, Mary. "Blue Sky Survey: Blue Sky in Deep Cyberspace: New Internet Research Resources for State Securities Law Practice." *The Business Lawyer*, November 1996 52 Bus. Law. 379.

5. Macek, Rosanne and Karen Draper. *Current Awareness at Bay Networks: Some Thoughts on Carbon-Based Filtering*, Karen Draper, Online World Conference '98, October 14, 1998. Tape and Presentation Slides.

6. Stratigos, Anthea and David Curle. *Putting the "I" back in CIO: The Changing Technical and Organizational Role of the Information Professional.* Outsell Inc. [http://www.outsellinc.com] (Contact Outsell, Inc., 345 California Drive, Suite 85, Burlingame, CA 94010, 650.342.7123, 650.342.7135 (Fax), Email: info@outsellinc.com).

7. Cleaver, Joanne. Careers: "What's Hot and What's Not," *Working Woman*, January 4, 1999 [http://www.workingwomanmag.com].

8. Buchanan, Leigh. "The Smartest Little Company in America," *Inc. Magazine*, January 1999, p. 42 [http://www.inc.com/incmagazine/archives/01990421.html].

9. Winzenreid, Arthur. "Towards 2006–Prophets, Princes or Poohbahs?" *Online & CDROM Review*, June 1997. (Also in *Online* November/December 1997, Logoff: After Thoughts compiled by Suzanne Bjorner, p. 112).

Wrap-Up:
Fourth International Conference on Fee-Based Information Services in Libraries

Suzanne M. Ward

The one-day pre-conference and the two-day meeting of the Fourth International Conference on Fee-Based Information Services in Libraries brought together information professionals from several countries and from all kinds of libraries. Some attendees had over a decade's experience managing fee-based services; others were only just beginning to grapple with the myriad issues for proposing that a service be established at their institutions. The conference met its goal of offering a range of speakers and breakout sessions that would appeal to the attendees no matter what their level of experience with fee-based services. The conference's other great accomplishment was to provide a forum for networking, for asking questions, and for exchanging both successful experiences and "war stories." Most fee-based service professionals feel somewhat isolated even if they work in a large institution, because most of their challenges and opportunities arc so different from those encountered by their local colleagues in more traditional library settings.

Library fee-based services are businesses in all but name, even if

---

Suzanne M. Ward is Head, Access Services, Purdue University Libraries.

[Haworth co-indexing entry note]: "Wrap-Up: Fourth International Conference on Fee-Based Information Services in Libraries." Ward, Suzanne M. Co-published simultaneously in *Journal of Interlibrary Loan, Document Delivery & Information Supply* (The Haworth Information Press, an imprint of The Haworth Press, Inc.) Vol. 10, No. 1, 1999, pp. 107-109; and: *Information Delivery in the 21st Century: Proceedings of the Fourth International Conference on Fee-Based Information Services in Libraries* (eds: Suzanne M. Ward, Yem S. Fong, and Tammy Nickelson Dearie) The Haworth Press, Inc., 1999, pp. 107-109. Single or multiple copies of this article are available for a fee from The Haworth Document Delivery Service [1-800-342-9678, 9:00 a.m. - 5:00 p.m. (EST). E-mail address: getinfo@haworthpressinc.com].

they operate on a non-profit basis, as most of them do. Managing a business-like unit in the midst of a larger, more traditional organization calls for equal parts of creativity and patience. Large organizations face change today, but smaller units like fee-based services must stay on the cutting edge to meet their customers' needs. In today's exploding information environment, businesspeople have a wide array of service providers to choose from, so library fee-based services work constantly to improve services for current clients and to attract potential customers. A responsive, well-managed operation that offers prompt, accurate, customized, and cost-effective information products often proves to be the best value a company can find for its information dollar.

The papers in this special issue represent about two-thirds of the sessions held at the conference. The wide ranging subjects, from copyright to pricing to the business environment, demonstrate the breadth of knowledge that a fee-based service manager needs to master. These managers must also acquire and practice a whole array of skills and competencies in order to be effective: technical expertise; personnel management; distribution channels; marketing; legal issues; traditional and non-traditional research methods; and strategic planning abilities. And it is no longer enough simply to acquire these skills once and coast. Managers of successful fee-based services constantly hone their skills and adapt them to the changing environment. One paper in this collection attests perfectly to this necessity; between the time she gave her paper at the conference in late 1997 and the time she wrote her article for this special issue in early 1999, Laura Gasaway completely revised her text to include changes in copyright compliance required by the 1998 Digital Millennium Copyright Act.

The conference's last session was a wrap-up in which the audience brainstormed first in small groups and then as a whole with the moderator to identify trends for fee-based information services. The group first looked at dying trends: Practices that are outdated or no longer relevant. Participants agreed that the days of reliance on print sources, manual procedures, and easy-to-find documents were over.

Next the audience identified established trends, those that currently comprise standard operating procedure. In this category people mentioned examples such as using the Web for research, declining institutional budgets for print material, and standard document delivery and research services.

Third, the participants thought of emerging trends, defined as experimental ideas gaining popularity. Examples mentioned included scanning documents for Web files, using online client ordering and tracking systems, and the impact of end-user searching.

Finally, the moderator led a discussion of boundary ideas, those radical approaches that are not yet accepted as good practice. The audience suggested "no limits" service, electronic hold shelves, and experience-based Web tools, among others.

The Fourth International Conference on Fee-Based Information Services in Libraries provided participants with several concentrated days in which to analyze current trends and developments in all phases of information delivery and to ponder the implications for the future. The conference helped participants identify the tools and skills they need to continue successfully serving their customers into the next decade and beyond.

Although separated at birth, both copies of Volume 2 exhibited identical foxing and mildew stains.

Index